Mirage Of Memories

A True Story…

Sweta Leena Panda

Copyright © <2024> <Sweta Leena Panda>

Dedication

To every woman who has ever questioned her path, who has given her heart and soul only to find herself standing alone. This is for those who have embraced kindness and simplicity, even when the world seemed to reward risk and ambition. Your strength, grace, and resilience, your unwavering spirit, are the heartbeat of this story. Let this novel be a reminder that the world's timeline does not define success, but by your courage to evolve, to take risks, and to transform your life. This is for you who choose love, success, or both, and sometimes, yourself above all.

Contents

Foreword

"Mirage of Memories" is an emotionally riveting narrative about one woman as she navigates her childhood, ambition, love, and loss through an intriguing life journey from rural Anji in Balasore near the DRDO centre to adult life in Rourkela steel city - perfectly depicting growing up with dreams that go far beyond small-town India.

As readers, we witness her unwavering determination as she pursues academic excellence at esteemed institutions like KIIT and IIT, her ambition to enter medicine, and the many schools and cities she visited along her path. Life, however, is not a straight path. After their college days at these two esteemed institutions were complete, she faced the harsh realities of adult life with its financial pressures and marital strife, eventually leading to divorce. Yet, she never lost her spirit, her resilience shining through every challenge.

"Mirage of Memories" is not just one woman's story but a reflection of many. It's a tale of how kindness can sometimes lead to unexpected outcomes. At 30, she finds herself alone and childless, reflecting on her journey. She grapples with society's expectations of success, love, and family life, a struggle many of us can relate to.

This novel delves deep into profound questions of identity and fulfilment. It explores our choices and the pursuit of personal success and meaning in life. At its core, it's a study of transformation- the courage to take risks and defy norms in the quest for personal fulfilment, even when life doesn't unfold as planned.

"Mirage of Memories" is an inspiring reminder that life doesn't always turn out how we expect; unexpected moments often lead us closer to discovering who we are and unlocking our true selves. The protagonist's journey is a testament to the power of self-discovery, urging us to reflect on our paths and the potential for personal growth that lies within unexpected twists and turns.

Name: Sweta Leena Panda

Date: 17.10.2024

Preface

Mirage of Memories invites readers to embark on an intimate journey into the life of a woman, from Anji to Pune. It's a journey that resonates with many, as she navigates the complexities of family, education, ambition, and love. The novel vividly portrays life's unpredictability, with its highs and lows, from childhood dreams of a medical career to the harsh realities of adulthood.

Set against her experiences at esteemed institutions like KIIT and IIIT, her journey reveals ambitions lost and found, from Bangalore to Maharashtra. The novel delves into the protagonist's personal battles, which culminate in an emotionally draining divorce process. Now at 30, she ponders society's expectations for marriage, children, and stability, and the pressure to conform to these norms. She finds herself single again, questioning the cost of kindness while trying to reconcile success and love.

At its core, this tale is a celebration of the protagonist's inner strength. It's a reminder that life necessitates taking risks, and the protagonist handles these challenges with equal ease. It's a story that empowers, showing that fulfilment can be found through self-transformation and inner strength, rather than just seeking external relief.

Author: Sweta Leena Panda

Date:17.10.2024

Acknowledgments

Mirage of Memories was an intensely personal endeavour for me, and its creation would not have happened without some amazing people in my life. To my family, who have always provided unconditional support throughout every stage of my life similarly mirroring what the protagonist goes through my most profound thanks go out as well to friends whose encouragement gave me strength in continuing this story of resilience and self-discovery; your trust gave me the energy I needed to continue writing Mirage of Memories!

Thank you to the women who have shared their tales of struggle, perseverance, and triumph with me. They have been such an essential source of motivation when creating this novel. Your strength and vulnerability serve as its core.

Finally, this book is dedicated to everyone who has bravely persevered through life's unexpected turns and made their journey forward despite it all. I want this work to prove that even through pain, self-reinvention, loneliness, or disappointment, there can still be strength, purpose, and eventual success waiting around the corner.

Thank you to all my readers for connecting with Mirage of Memories; your participation makes the tale come to life!

FINDING HOME WITHIN MYSELF

The rain tracks silver across the windowpane and echoes in the quiet of a hundred grey airport skies. In this calm, still moment, usually accompanied by the hum of the departure gate and roar of flying, I experience a profound silence. It's like a convergent. It is a feeling that each turn and every stumble, as well as every moment of happiness, has been a compass line that led me here, at the edge of a city I had never heard of until this day. The city's skyline is a pencil sketch of a bleak sunset; its pulsing heartbeat sounds like a string of foreign words. There is no place I've been yet, and I've never felt more clearly me.

> *"We were not created with an exact map, but rather with a rhythm. It is when we follow that pulse, even if it is a little shaky, that we can find our real north."*

My story doesn't begin with the stamp of a passport. It starts with the stunning, chaotic world of my childhood, when the world seemed vast and complex. I was always on the hunt for missing parts, attempting to make a tidy image out of the fragments. Resilience was not a word I knew at the time. It was simply the desire to get up after falling and to see a flicker of light in the dark space, to keep moving even when the path disappeared under my feet. That girl, who worked constantly sifting through the wreckage, was creating an underlying foundation for the person who sits in a foreign sunset.

I've come to realise that belonging isn't a matter of individual postal codes. It's not just the ground under the feet of your shoes; it is rather the muscle in your bones, forged by battle, then tempered by triumph, and shaped with those instances of pure awe-inspiring joy. It's the profound realisation that, even in the most solitary of places, you can be at home if you truly know yourself.

The journey I am on is not a series of steps, but a deep dive. It's a search for memories that are both tender and complex, the seemingly impossible challenges that eventually became the foundation of my power, the pleasures that now hurt with their sweet awe. To fully comprehend the person looking at this rain, it is first necessary to be with the child who was taught to walk without knowing the exact destination.

I was once an unresolved outcast, a shadow against any backdrop. Today, I realise that home was always a changing frontier. It's what's next, the following step, or the brave opening of an entrance. The child that was lost is there, but not as a ghost, but instead as a compass, her tiny hand in mine, whispering to me that this way serves the goal.

The next chapter will be waiting on the tarmac, amid the buzz of an engine from a jet. Every great story needs a solid foundation. Therefore, let's rewind the movie. We'll go back to the beginning, back to the spot where the puzzle first dropped on the floor. I encourage you to stroll with me through these pages to study the basic materials of strength and the quietly powerful act of self-discovery.

Your role as a reader is not inactive. It's essential. Each story requires witnesses, and as it is shared, the story, like a raindrop reaching the ground, finds its perfect shape.

Threads of My Journey

A JOURNEY FROM VILLAGE TO VISION

My roots run deep in Anji, a village nestled between the Bay of Bengal and ancient banyans, five kilometres from the ocean, 20 minutes from port, yet worlds away from everyday life. There, I learned to balance my parents' legacy with what could become mine; my journey began under its shadow.

Life at Anji wasn't lived by mere minutes and moments, but rather in the moments. The hum of palms created the soundtrack to my childhood: the faint hum of a boat's engine cutting through the salty air, and the pulsing, predawn call of the Shiva temple, which sank into the wall space like a beat. The time didn't move, and it swayed. It moved at the speed of the reflection in the pond, shifting with the light, but despite it all, it remained completely still.

Our house was in the ethereal gaze of this ancient temple. This spire served as my first navigational; its shadow was a cool, dark line across our yard every afternoon. It was a constant reminder of something bigger than us. Being so close to God was considered a gift. The air smelled of incense and calm, punctuated by the copper bell of my church. My consistent and gentle connection with him not only changed my prayer practice but also altered my taste preferences, teaching me that food can serve more than one purpose: it can act as a means to remember and express reverence for Him.

"In the shadow of the temple I was taught the first recipe for faith: that it as well as flavour must be nurtured with silence before being given to others."

Our natural surroundings were our vivacious, untamed partner. Two massive banyan trees stood guard over our house, with roots that resembled broken ropes hanging from the skies, their canopy providing a space for chattering birds as well as inquisitive spirits. Under them, I sensed the profound, humble realisation that my story was a mere thread in a massive, living tapestry. Our ponds were like liquid sky, with clouds forming by day, and glistening with thousands of stars at night. They were alive, from silvery fish to the sudden, exciting sightings of kingfishers on their way to the ocean and a flash of blue lightning in the midst of everyday life.

However, this paradise was not without its serpents, literal ones. They would pop up, smooth and abrupt, in an area of the verandah or near the well, releasing an adrenaline rush into the tranquil. My father, who was calm and steady, would tell me, "Do not fear. They are the protectors of Lord Shiva. Every creature has a home in this world." His voice was so clear that I learned the lesson that would eventually be the foundation of my kitchen: to respect each ingredient, know its essence, and be afraid can turn into fascination.

They were my parents' bridge to an old world and the pulsation of a contemporary one. My father, who had an MSc in Mathematical Sciences, spoke of numbers as if they were hearts and tales. My mother, who had an MA in Political Science, analysed human narratives with the same accuracy. Their union was a tradition that began on the 26th of June in 1989 and, in the rural background of Anji, grew into a profound, loving, conscious relationship. Being able to watch a woman born in the city like my mother figure out her rhythm within the rhythms of the village, mastering cooking in the oven made of clay, figuring out what the mood of the monsoon is to do the laundry, but not losing her intellect, was my first experience of adaptation. In her resiliency, I was able to see the future.

And then there was my grandfather, the landlord and storyteller, as well as the bedrock. The time he had was his stage. He would sip his tea, his eyes watering, and tell tales of his forefathers travelling on donkeys as well as palkis to collect rents of vast land areas where one could walk for many days. His stories were epic, but his life at the moment was straightforward. That juxtaposition of grandeur in narrative and simplicity in practice seared itself into me.

"My great-grandfather's legacy wasn't in the land he owned; however, it was in the stories that he told with tea, a reminder that even the simplest of vessels can be used to hold the strongest beverage."

The man who taught me was that real strength doesn't lie in dominance and control, but in leadership. This ambition may cause you to rise; however, only your roots can keep you standing in the storm. In his accounts of managing life and land, I came across guidelines for managing flavours by establishing authority and exercising great care to ensure that every aspect achieves its full potential.

When I sit at my table, the aromas that emanate aren't only of tempering oil and spices. They're the scent of incense from temples early in the morning, of damp soil after the first rain, and of my mum's sweat, and the determination to keep going over the flame of the newspaper that my father's calculations became poetry. Every meal I cook is a page from this book, a moment from my personal cinematic memories.

Anji was much more than an environment; it was the main ingredient. An area where snakes ruled and ponds provided views of the sky; temple shadows indicated a young girl serving up her meal as an offering - just as an ideal scenario should include both tradition and innovation, respect for all parties involved, and confidence from its residents as a foundation to reach beyond.

SHIFTS IN RESPONSIBILITIES

The death of my grandmother at age fifty was not a personal loss. The cause was an earthquake that triggered a fault line cutting through the bedrock, permanently changing who we were. The absence of her was a quiet heavy stone that fell in the middle of our lives. And the ripples that they created and rearranged were never completely settled. "We believed we had lost an entire heart in that moment," I would later write, "but we didn't realise that the entire body would lose what it was like to be beat."

After the shock, the roles were split and transformed. My grandfather, who had a profound faith and was a quiet one, was not merely grieving. He sought refuge. The solution to the gruelling calculation of the loss of one soul away was to subtract his own from the everyday equation. He picked Puri, the city of sacred significance near the sea, not as a destination to visit, but as a place where the possibility of disappearing exists. He travelled to Puri to purify himself, seek refuge in the pulsing crash of waves against temple stones, and immerse himself in the rituals of devotion associated with Puri. Puri Mutt. It was a solemn exchange of responsibility: the passing of the family lantern from his hand to my grandmother's torch in my father's, a burden accepted, however, not without an elongated stomp.

Puri is to become his place of refuge. The final scene in a lifetime of spiritual growth. He imagined his final years as a lengthy and slow exhale of prayers and service. But it appears that fate is an unforgiving director. The script was changed.

The call came in an ordinary night with the kind of peaceful evening that can make the breaking of peace seem so complete. The night we had dinner; my father suddenly grew nervous during a tense phone call. It resulted in a shift from his regular, calm face, which reflected on us, to an unsettling crimson cloud, and then to a return to the bluish-black clarity. "There must have been something wrong," the voice on the line had told my father before abruptly hanging up - words which could never honestly be held within any one person's grasp; "something was definitely amiss". Was something amiss here? Or had something gone terribly amiss here?

On a pilgrimage excursion to Delhi, my grandfather fell, a sudden, violent stroke. The fellow devotees discovered him unconscious, and he was rushed to an unreachable hospital far away. The man who sought the Divine on his own was frightened, trapped in a medical room.

The following sequence of events was my father's desperate attempt to get him back: the long, quiet drive towards Rourkela, with a spectre of the guy he knew. Our home, which was still sounding the loss of my grandmother, was now subject to another, more intense change. It was transformed overnight into an open-air hospital. The antiseptic flavour of the medicine tempered the familiar aroma of spices. The bedroom converted into a shackle of humankind, filled with monitors that traced the rough ground of his existence.

The grandfather who came back was only a shaky echo. The stroke had altered his body's language. It left his body weak, and his speech was slurred and dependent on him for basic actions. In this harsh new light, our family portrait changed and revealed a strength we hadn't realised we possessed.

My mother was the general of our camp; as such, she oversaw medicines and doctors with great diligence and precision. My brother and I served as assistants to her camp, providing water, sips of refreshment, hours of companionship, and helping my father take hospital visits and discuss details with his friends in private conversations, while his shoulders eventually gave out under the burden. We made our way through the world by installing rails and making room for a wheelchair, and each change was a silent prayer made of wood and steel.

It was exhausting, a constant audition for roles that we had never dreamed of. The idea of seeing a patriarch reduced to a man who ate a spoonful of food, whom you once took up to the heavens, is a painful experience. In the midst of that struggle, an excruciating beauty emerged. It was no longer a bloodline bound by blood or name. We became a group that was battling for survival in the same tidal wave. Our love was tangible, as the bed was adjusted, the hair brushed, and the night watch maintained.

The subject matter in films of our lives shifted from being an account of loss to an intimate, sombre story of love. Close-ups replaced the wide image of our bonds with family, such as my father's hand, holding the cup in a twitch while my mother's eyes scanned a health chart, and that tiny, hard-earned smile of my grandfather's when he spotted an old tune. The music was the sounds of the oxygen concentrator and the tempo of our new breaths.

We lost the bedrock of my grandmother's house, and his lighthouse. However, in the desperate struggle to stop his flame from shining, we discovered that we had constructed a new foundation, not made of stone, but of intertwined hands. It was cracked and soft, but strong enough to hold. The family that the grief was breaking, as well as the devotion that was a different, more grinding kind, started to bind back together more strongly in its fractured locations.

THE BLEND OF TRADITION AND ASPIRATION

My father's career in the railway industry caused us to move frequently across town, to Sini, CKP, and Ranchi, before settling in Rourkela for a few decades.

Sini was where my adventure began. It was a small city awash with beautiful vegetation and endless railway tracks that stretched to the sky. As a youngster, I was captivated by the constant hum of the tracks close to our house, where I watched my parents adjust quickly to their brand-new family and community. Their resilience was genuinely fantastic to me, as they quickly made adjustments and lived a life utterly different from the one, they had experienced before moving to this area.

Chakradharpur (CKP), a bustling railway town famous for its lively markets and diverse population, was our next stop. It was like entering a different world that was full of exciting adventures!

Ranchi was a pivotal stop in our travels, a significant turning point due to its top-tier educational institutions and its rich traditional culture. I was tangled in the middle of childhood bliss and unfulfilled dreams.

Rourkela was not just another spot on our map. It provided stability to our family and the opportunity to fulfil our goals here. After a long time living in different railway towns with diverse cultures and rhythms, Rourkela provided the stability we had always wanted and had been lacking before.

Each move was unique. When we moved into our new home, there was always an initial phase of adjustment in which I had to master the new school curriculum quickly, find new friends, and simultaneously maintain my academic standards. However, regardless of our housing arrangements, I did my best academically.

Each of the towns we lived in left a mark on me, whether through friendships formed or lessons learned outside the classroom. These experiences opened my eyes and helped me appreciate India's cultural diversity.

Rourkela brought new academic rigour and personal growth for us. We moved into a modest home near our school, which is known for its steel mill and vibrant community life. We were able to experience activities that were unlike those we had at home. Every turn was filled with hope of new successes ahead.

Rourkela offered both stimulating and challenging learning experiences. The rigorous curriculum and competitive atmosphere are distinctly different from my experiences in rural India. Therefore, the ability to adapt and be resilient is essential to my quest for excellence.

When I was in school in Rourkela, I was constantly receiving awards. Being named Best Student from fifth grade through ninth grade demonstrated my commitment; these accomplishments inspired me to become a doctor after observing how highly regarded they were within my family.

My school days were characterised by my insatiable curiosity and accomplishments in a variety of areas. For example, from Math Olympiads, where I competed against some of the best minds, and art competitions, which let me express my imagination without words, each encounter added an essential layer to my academic journey.

Mathematics was my primary discipline for developing my mathematical thinking. Art competitions let my imagination run wild. Poetry recitation or painting events let me express my emotions or thoughts that words could not convey. One of my favourite memories is writing poems in Sanskrit (a spoken language that sounded like music to my ears) and seeing them published in the school's magazine.

While I sat in the tranquillity and peace of my home, the ancient banyan trees that whispered stories and the serene lakes that reflected their vastness, I discovered my passion for writing poems in Sanskrit. With its extensive and prestigious tradition, the language of classical times allowed me to express my feelings and thoughts that transcended the realm of everyday life.

My path to poetry began out of pure curiosity. Chants from the Shiva temple close to our home were often heard in our house. I was captivated by their mellow cadence, which prompted me to write poetry that portrayed the beauty of life and beauty through language. Each poem was an experiment to capture short-lived moments or timeless truths through words.

The accolades I received during my early years not only increased my self-confidence but also reinforced my determination to become a doctor. The ability to see in person how respected doctors were within the community motivated me to seek a profession, and I aimed not only to look attractive but also to create tangible changes in the lives of others, especially those less fortunate than I am.

The Best Student Award served more than just as an award. It also motivated me, reminding me that every goal can be accomplished by perseverance and determination.

My family was strong during this time of struggle, and especially my father, who pushed us to be better and was proud of each report card we handed in, despite his hectic work at the train station. He was always supportive of our academic activities, even during late-night studies or report card reviews.

During this time, I learned valuable lessons in persistence, determination, passion, and gratitude that will help me through future challenges.

The ninth summer I spent with my family was memorable because we faced one of the most difficult family challenges, which tested our resilience and unity within an extended family. My grandpa was diagnosed with an injury on a trip to Delhi. He was hospitalised, which brought our strength under severe stress as we had to navigate medical visits and routines as a unit of family.

The family members felt extremely stressed throughout this time. My brother and I attempted to keep a balance between schoolwork and caring obligations while maintaining peace and calm. The result was that this chaos caused my school to suffer, as the hum of medical equipment and discussions on health-related issues took place behind locked doors.

My father quickly recognised the strain on my academic performance, and to ensure I was healthy and educated, I signed up at KIIT to establish a place where I could concentrate on my studies, free from interruptions or distractions. Although it was a bit daunting at first because of my lack of experience in the environment, it eventually became a place where my academic goals could grow while also teaching me independence.

The experience of attending boarding school was unforgettable. An intimate group of kids from diverse backgrounds living together in a single space. While it was at first challenging to adapt, the structured atmosphere allowed me to focus my efforts effectively while still preserving my family's values.

My First Hostel Life

"We build our castles of dreams with the fragile bricks of hope, only to learn that the hardest lessons come from those we invite across the drawbridge."

THE CASTLE OF SOLITUDE – YEAR OF THE DREAMER

The walls of my childhood home were painted in shades of quiet love and profound solitude. I was an only child in a colony where time moved with the languid pace of old trees, and there were no other souls my age to share the peculiar turbulence of growing up. My days were a predictable sequence: school, homework, the gentle but watchful eyes of my parents, and the echoing silence of evenings where my own thoughts were my loudest companions. I was not unhappy, not in the dramatic sense. I was cushioned by care, but I was starving for a world that buzzed, for a life that felt shared, for stories that were not just mine to tell. I felt like a bird in a very comfortable, gilded cage, singing a song only I could hear the depth of.

So, when the possibility of hostel life emerged, it didn't feel like a mere change of address. It felt like the universe was finally handing me the key to my own destiny. The word "hostel" itself shimmered with a mythical glow. It promised a symphony of chattering voices down long corridors, the conspiratorial whispers of late-night conversations, the sacred bond of a sisterhood forged in the fires of shared independence. Most of all, it promised freedom. Freedom from the kindly but constant scrutiny of parents who, with the best intentions, judged every deviation from their path. No one to scold me for reading past midnight. No one to question my choices. I could be the architect of my own days, the author of my own nights. The excitement was physical, a flutter in my stomach that lasted for weeks. I drafted elaborate, mental blueprints for my new life. I would be studious but social, disciplined but fun. I would collect friends like treasures.

The arrival at the hostel was a sensory overload of newness, the smell of fresh paint and anxiety, the cacophony of parents advising, trunks scraping, and girls tentatively greeting one another. Amidst this whirlwind, I made my first, defining decision: I chose a single room. It was an act of profound self-knowledge, even if I couldn't articulate it then. At home, I had craved noise, but for the sacred act of studying, I required a sanctuary. I could not concentrate in a crowd; my mind was like a delicate vessel that spilt its contents amidst chaos. A single room would be my library, my thinking chamber, the cockpit from where I would steer my ambitious flight towards medical school.

This choice became a spectacle for the visiting parents. They would peer into my small, neat room, then at me, a girl who looked younger than her years, with a mixture of confusion and concern. Their questions were variations on a theme: "Why alone?" "Aren't you scared?" "What will you do if you feel afraid at night?" I smiled politely, offering feeble assurances, but inside, a slight doubt began to gnaw. Was my self-awareness being mistaken for weakness? Was my sanctuary going to be my prison of loneliness?

And then, he appeared. An uncle of one of my future friends, a man with a calm, surveying gaze that seemed to look past the surface. He stood at my doorway, not with pity, but with a curious appreciation. He joked, his eyes crinkling, "What will you do at night if you get scared, or if a ghost decides to visit?" Before I could muster a defensive reply, his expression softened into one of pure respect. "I think you are a brave girl," he said, and the words landed in my heart with the weight of truth. "It's good you chose a single room. Even I loved to read alone. In my PG time, I chose a single room, and after that… I got my IAS. So try your best to fulfil your dream. My blessing is with you."

Tears. Immediate, unbidden, and healing. They didn't fall from sadness, but from a powerful sense of being *seen*. He had looked at my choice and seen not fear, but fortitude; not isolation, but ambition. He had reflected to me the proudest, most hopeful version of myself I carried inside. That blessing wasn't just a polite phrase; it was a mantle laid on my shoulders. My single room transformed in that instant. It was no longer just a room; it was a castle. And I was its queen, ruling over kingdoms of biology textbooks and chemistry equations, my dreams flying like banners from its imagined turrets.

The social life I had yearned for blossomed in the fertile ground just outside my castle walls. The girls in the adjacent rooms became my chosen family. My innate shyness melted in the warmth of shared experiences. We were all novices in this art of self-governance, and there was comedy in our failures, the disastrous attempts at washing clothes, the clandestine midnight feasts of maggi. I spent so much time laughing in their rooms that the stern lady attendant would often shoo me back to my own quarters during official study hours. "You are disturbing the serious ones!" she'd scold, but her eyes held a twinkle. I was collecting friendships; each one a glowing gem I believed was priceless and permanent. I trusted with the open, foolish heart of someone who has never been truly betrayed.

The first year was a sweet, uncomplicated sonnet. Then, as the sky darkened with the approach of first-year final exams, a request came that would change the melody. She was my bench-mate, a girl with intelligent eyes and a perpetual slight frown of concentration. One day, her scowl deepened with distress. "My roommate," she whispered, leaning close, "she plays music all night. She is… unbearable. I cannot study. Could I… could I possibly stay with you? Just until the exams are over?"

My heart expanded with purpose. Exams were sacred; the solidarity of stress was a bond I understood deeply. How could I refuse a scholar in need? This was my chance to be not just a friend, but a saviour. "Of course," I said, without a moment's hesitation. I opened the heavy door of my castle, and she walked in.

Our days developed a new, purposeful rhythm. I would study my own portions, then, patiently and meticulously, turn to hers. She was bright but struggled with mathematics and chemistry. I would break down complex problems into tiny, digestible steps. I taught her the way I wished someone had sometimes taught me with patience, with analogies, with relentless encouragement. For three, sometimes four hours each evening, my room was a tiny tutoring school. And I loved it. Teaching was my love language. It made me feel capable, helpful, and connected. At home, I taught my younger brother and cousins, and here, I could extend that part of myself. I saw her grasp a concept, her face lighting up with understanding, and it felt like a personal victory. I was investing not just time, but emotional capital. I was building a friendship on the bedrock of shared intellectual struggle.

The exams ended. We went home for vacation, carrying the relief of survivors. Returning, we were met with momentous news: our new, permanent hostel on campus was ready. We were to choose our roommates for the year that truly mattered, our final board exam year.

She found me immediately. "We have to stay together," she said, her hand on my arm. "We work so well. We're from the same section, and we understand the pressure. My last roommate was a nightmare. I need someone like you." Her words were flattering, a validation of my helpful nature. And there was another girl, one with a smile so genuine it could disarm the sternest teacher, an innocence about her that felt like a cool cloth on a fevered brow. I loved talking to her; her presence was peaceful. I chose them. This would be my new, permanent family a trio of ambition and amity.

But the room itself was our first collective disappointment. It was a grim, architectural afterthought, facing a direction where the sun was a reluctant visitor. The light that did enter was weak and grey, dying before it reached my assigned bed in the corner. I was a creature of sunlight. I needed it like oxygen, its warmth a physical comfort for my often-ailing spirit. This gloom was a physical weight. And my spirit, it seemed, was already buckling.

I had entered hostel life intellectually prepared but domestically inept. I was a terrible steward of my own body. I ate when I remembered, slept erratic hours, and when the inevitable hostel bugs made their rounds, I played a dangerous, arrogant game of doctor. My father, worried for his distant daughter, had given me a small pharmacy of general medicines for fever, for cough, for aches. I treated them like sweets, popping pills based on hunches, not symptoms. My body, a finely tuned instrument, began to rebel in cacophony.

The first fractures in our trio appeared subtly, like thin cracks in ice. One horrific night, the innocent one, the girl with the gentle smile, was violently, terrifyingly ill. One moment she was fine, the next she was curled over, vomiting uncontrollably, her skin burning to the touch. Panic seized me. I turned to my other roommate, the one I'd tutored, the one I'd chosen. "Help me," I pleaded. "We need to get her water, a cold cloth…"

She took one look, a hand flying to her own mouth, and recoiled into her bedsheets. "Don't! Please don't call me. If I see it, I'll vomit too. I can't." And she turned her face to the wall.

The rejection was a slap. But the sick girl moaned, and there was no time for hurt feelings. Alone, fighting my own visceral revulsion, I cleaned up. I held her hair, wiped her face, and placed a wobbly bucket beside her bed. The smell was awful, a sour, invasive presence in the dark room. I breathed through my mouth, tears of strain and disgust in my eyes. I stayed awake until dawn broke, listening to her ragged breathing, feeling utterly alone in a room with two other people.

The betrayal, however, was a seed planted in the dark, and it sprouted in the morning's cruel light. From the bathroom, I heard her sweet, concerned voice talking to our recovered friend. "Oh, I'm so, so sorry I couldn't help you last night. She never even woke me! If I'd known, I would have been right there." The lie was delivered with such convincing regret. A coldness settled in my gut, different from the nausea of the night before. This was a calculated rewriting of history. It was my first authentic taste of a poison that leaves no taste at all.

What followed was a slow, terrifying unravelling of my own self. A profound, bone-deep fatigue began to claim me. It wasn't ordinary tiredness; it was a drowning sensation. I would sleep for ten, eleven hours and wake up feeling as if I'd run a marathon. My body was a prison of lead. My mind, once sharp and eager, was swaddled in thick fog. The two most important years of my academic life, my board exams and my medical entrance preparation, loomed like twin executioners, but I could barely lift my head from the pillow. I attended classes like a ghost, sitting in the first row but seeing nothing, hearing nothing. When the fog became too thick, I would stumble to the last row and surrender, sleeping through lectures on biology, chemistry, and my own future. The side effects of the strong allopathic medicines I was now haphazardly taking for my persistent, worsening illnesses only deepened the stupor.

My academic performance, my pride, crumbled into dust. The monthly test results were a horror show. In mathematics, my strongest subject, where I used to score above 25 out of 30 consistently, I stared at a paper marked "8". The shame was a hot, choking thing. My mathematics teacher, a woman who had often smiled at me with approval, called me to the front of the class. Her disappointment was a physical force. "What is this?" she hissed, holding up my paper. "Is this the best you can do? You should be ashamed. You are wasting your talent. Leave the class if this is the effort you will make."

The words carved into me. I stood there, my head bowed, the weight of my failing body and my failing grades threatening to bring me to my knees. After class, I stumbled to her, the truth tumbling out in a tearful, broken stream: the illness, the fatigue, the medicine. Her face transformed from anger to shock, then to a deep, maternal concern. She promised extra help, her hand on my shoulder a fleeting anchor. But the damage to my confidence was done.

My most desperate attempt to reclaim control was setting an alarm for 4 AM. I would put it with a ritualistic hope, placing it far from my bed so I'd have to get up to silence it. But every morning, without fail, I awoke at 6:30, disoriented and defeated. The alarm was silent. I blamed myself for my drugged, heavy sleep. "I must have switched it off in my sleep," I'd groan. I begged my roommates, "Please, if you hear it at 4, shake me awake. It's life or death for me." They would nod, but every morning was the same. They'd say, "You probably did it yourself. You're like a zombie these days."

Then came the night that shattered the last illusion. I awoke at that witching hour of 4 AM. I was drowsy, but conscious. The room was pitch black, filled with the rhythmic breathing of sleep. And then I saw it, a silhouette detaching itself from a bed. It moved silently to my desk. A faint, green glow from the alarm clock illuminated her face for a second. It was her. My friend. My tutor. My chosen roommate. With a deliberate, precise movement, she pressed the buttons, changing the time. Then, with a final, soft *click*, she switched the alarm off entirely. She stood there for a moment, a shadow against the deeper dark, then drifted back to her bed.

The world did not spin; it froze. There was no sound but the deafening roar of blood in my ears, the cracking of my naive heart. I did not move. I did not breathe. Tears, silent and scalding, seeped from the corners of my eyes, tracing a cold path into my hair and onto the pillow. This was not a mistake. This was not sleepwalking. This was a conscious, calculated act of sabotage. She had seen me struggle, seen me drown, and instead of throwing a rope, she had quietly pushed my head back under.

Morning came, a grotesque pantomime. She stretched, yawned, and saw me already sitting up. Her voice was a masterpiece of counterfeit surprise. "Oh! Look who's up! How did *you* manage to wake up so early, my sleeping beauty?" The endearment was a knife twisted in the wound.

I carried the corrosive truth inside me all day. Finally, alone with her, my voice trembling with a mixture of hurt and fury, I confronted her. "I saw you. Last night. You changed my alarm."

Her transformation was instant and chilling. The sweet mask dissolved into cold denial. "What are you talking about? You're hallucinating. The medicine is affecting your brain." She said it with such conviction, such pitying disdain. Then, she took her story public. I heard her in the standard room, speaking to a cluster of girls. "Poor thing, she's so stressed she's seeing things now. She accused me of the strangest stuff. I'm worried about her mental state." The strategy was brilliant and brutal: not just deny, but discredit. To save herself from a minor accusation, she was willing to paint me as unstable.

The pain was absolute. It was a death, the death of trust, the death of a particular kind of hope. I could fight illness. I could fight failing grades. But how do you fight a lie that paints you as the liar? How do you defend a reality someone is systematically erasing?

My response was one of silent, profound retreat. I bought a cheap, floral-patterned screen and hung it around my bed. It was a flimsy barrier of cloth, but it was my Berlin Wall. It created a tiny, sovereign nation of one. Behind it, I studied in fierce, isolated silence. I set multiple, hidden alarms. I spoke only when necessary. The message was clear: *You are banished from my spirit.* She pleaded, her performances of wounded friendship now meaningless to me. "Why are you doing this? We're friends!" But the bridge was not just burned; it was reduced to ash scattered by the wind.

The final months of that year were a grim marathon of survival. Broken in health and heart, I finally fled home for a brief study leave. There, in the embrace of my worried family, I surrendered my broken body to the gentle, systemic wisdom of homeopathy and Ayurveda. The strong allopathic pills had been a sledgehammer; these were like skilled surgeons, carefully stitching me back together, molecule by molecule. My energy began a slow, tentative return. The fog in my mind lifted, leaving behind the stark, clear landscape of all I had lost and all I had to recover.

I returned to sit for my final board exams, a wounded soldier with only a few weeks of actual, clear-headed preparation. I had entered the hostel as a dreamer, armed with blueprints for a palace of friendship and success. I left the first chapter of that life carrying the bricks of my own broken castle, each one heavy with the mortar of betrayal, illness, and a hard-won, painful wisdom. I had learned that not every open door should be entered, and not every extended hand intends to pull you up. Sometimes, they are there to measure the distance of your fall.

24

THE FORTRESS & THE STAGE – YEAR OF THE SURVIVOR

The girl who returned to the hostel for her final year was a different creature. The wide-eyed dreamer of Chapter One had been folded up and put away, like a childish drawing. In her place stood a young woman whose eyes held a new, watchful depth. The steady, gentle rhythms of homoeopathy and Ayurveda had subdued the chaos of my health. My body was no longer the enemy; it was a convalescent, slowly regaining strength. But if my physical walls were being repaired, the emotional ones had been rebuilt higher, thicker, and with narrow, careful windows. Trust was no longer a gift I offered freely; it was a scarce currency, earned in small, painstaking increments.

The innocence was gone. The belief that friendship was an automatic, permanent state had been incinerated. I moved through the hostel routines with a polite, purposeful detachment. I was cordial with my roommate, the one who had switched the alarm, but a vast, Arctic tundra existed between us, frozen over by her lie and my silent knowledge of it. Our interactions were transactions: "Pass the salt." "The light is off." The vibrant, tutoring-filled connection was dead, and I felt no desire to resuscitate it. I had learned a brutal economics of the heart: some investments yield only bankruptcy.

Yet, life, in its stubborn insistence on balance, had left me with a precious asset. The other girl, the one with the innocent smile who had been so ill that night, remained. Our friendship, forged in the quiet aftermath of that drama, deepened. She had seen the tension, heard the whispers, and chosen to believe the silent truth of my character over the spoken falsehoods. She became my oasis. In our shared corner of the room, behind the mental safety of my screen, we built a small world of sanity. We exchanged notes, not just academic ones, but emotional ones. We whispered about our fears for the future, the overwhelming pressure of the approaching exams, the silly, gossiped-about crushes on boys in the coaching classes. She never asked me to take down my screen; she understood it was my armour. Her presence was a constant, gentle warmth, a proof that not all light could be extinguished by one act of shadow. We spoke of becoming doctors, of the lives we would lead, of making a difference. Her faith in me was a quiet, steady stream that helped irrigate the parched fields of my self-belief.

And then, there was the most unexpected, beautiful subplot of my survival story: Him. My best friend. This was not a romantic love story in the conventional, sweeping sense. It was a love story of the soul. It was a biography of two similar texts finding each other in a chaotic library. We met not with a crash of cymbals, but with the quiet click of recognition in the dusty silence of the college library, over shared frustration with a particularly vicious physics problem in the canteen. He was calm where I was stormy, logical where I was emotional, wryly observant where I was passionately immersed. With him, I didn't have to dissect the pain of the hostel. He seemed to sense it, a current beneath my words. He never pressed for details; he simply offered a solid, unwavering presence. He was my sanctuary *outside* the hostel walls. In the small tea shop near our coaching institute, over cups of too-sweet chai, the weight of my vigilance would lift. I could set down the burden of being "the girl who was cheated" or "the sick one" and just be a student, a dreamer, a person who could laugh until her sides hurt.

His love was in the actions: the photocopied notes from a class I'd missed due to a check-up, slipped to me without comment; the fierce, protective scowl he'd get when someone mentioned my former roommate's name in a positive light; the simple, steadfast belief that I would not just pass, but excel. "You're the smartest person I know," he'd say, not as flattery, but as a simple statement of fact. It was an ambitious love, one that believed in my future as fervently as I was struggling to. He was the beautiful, necessary counterpoint to the betrayal, living proof that loyalty and kindness were not myths.

The academic pressure of the final year was a tangible, suffocating presence. It was the air we breathed, thick with anxiety and ambition. But now, I was fighting back with a focused, cold fury. The single-room discipline, once a choice for concentration, had become a non-negotiable survival skill. I honed the art of concentrated isolation. I learned to say "no" to distractions, to guard my study hours with the ferocity of a she-wolf protecting her den. My health, while better, was still fragile. I had to be the meticulous doctor to myself that I had failed to be before regulating sleep, eating correctly, and taking my homoeopathic doses on time. This self-care was no longer a chore; it was a strategic campaign.

Amidst this grim landscape of revision and resistance, life offered a chance for pure, unadulterated joy at the Annual College Comedy and Science Exhibition. It was a callback to the fearless, participatory girl I had been, the one who existed before the betrayal. On a whim, fuelled by a nostalgia for that simpler self, I signed up. I teamed up with a classmate for a chemistry-based project, something involving a dramatic colour-change reaction. The concept was thrilling. Then came the obstacle: it required a specific, rare, and moderately poisonous chemical salt. It was expensive, and the college lab, citing safety, refused to provide it.

My partner's courage evaporated. "It's too risky. What if we get in trouble? What if it goes wrong? I'm out," she said, and just like that, I was alone again. Old me would have crumpled, seen it as a sign to give up. But the new me, the survivor, felt a different fire, a stubborn, defiant spark. "By hook or by crook," I muttered to myself, a new personal mantra, "I will do this."

For two days, I was a portrait of frantic paralysis. Everyone else's models and experiments were taking shape around me. I had nothing but an empty table and a sinking heart. In desperation, I approached my Chemistry professor, the stern but fair lab-in-charge. I laid out my case, my voice trembling but clear. I showed him my detailed plans, my safety precautions. I saw him weigh my desperation against the rules. Finally, he sighed. "Alright. But you are solely responsible. And you must have a partner for safety. No working alone."

A partner. The very thing I lacked. As I walked out of his office, feeling a flicker of hope, I literally bumped into another girl in the corridor. She was clutching a half-built model of a volcano, and her face was streaked with tears of frustration. We stammered apologies, and in that moment of mutual distress, our stories tumbled out. Her partner, too, had abandoned her at the last minute. We stared at each other, and in that shared look of panic and determination, a partnership was born. We were a duo of the desperate and the determined.

What followed was the most glorious, chaotic night of my college life. One night. One single, sleepless night to build two exhibitions from scratch. We commandeered a corner of the empty lab. My chemistry was combined with her geology in a wild, improvised synergy. We worked with a frenetic, laughing energy, fuelled by cold coffee and a shared, giddy sense of rebellion. She helped me measure my precise amounts of toxic powders. I helped her paint her papier-mâché volcano. We argued over the circuit connections for her lava lamp effect and debated the best way to present my chemical clock reaction. It was creative madness, a storm of glue, wires, and sudden breakthroughs. At 4 AM, covered in paint and exhaustion, we looked at our completed projects, her erupting volcano, my precise array of glassware, and high-fived like conquerors. We had built something from nothing.

The next morning, bleary-eyed but buzzing with triumph, we presented our work in the exhibition hall. The judges came, asked questions, and nodded approvingly. A flush of pride warmed me. Then came the twist. As the first wave of visiting students and parents began to stream into the hall, I had to dash across campus to the auditorium. My comedy skit was about to begin.

My hostel friends, who knew my history of stage fright and my tendency to weep under pressure, told me later they had formed a prayer huddle. "We were literally begging any god who would listen," my innocent roommate laughed, "'Please, don't let her freeze. Don't let her cry on stage!

I stood in the wings, my heart pounding a frantic rhythm against my ribs. The memories of betrayal, illness, and loneliness flashed not as fears, but as fuel. I had faced darker things than a spotlight. I had been betrayed in the intimate dark of a shared room. This was just light. This was just an audience. I walked onto the stage. The lights were blinding, hot. I took a breath, found my best friend's face in the third row, he gave me a solemn, encouraging nod, and I began.

I delivered my lines. I timed the pauses. A chuckle rippled through the crowd. Then a louder laugh. Then a roar. I was doing it. I was making them laugh. The applause that followed as I took my bow wasn't just for a comedy act; it was a thunderous affirmation. It was the sound of a spirit, once crushed, finding its voice again and discovering it could sing, it could shout, it could command joy. I had not cried. I had shone.

The final weeks were a blur of last-minute revisions and sentimental goodbyes. I sat for my board exams in a state of calm focus I hadn't known was possible. The ordeal had tempered me. When I finally left the hostel gates for the last time, my trunk was lighter, but my soul was heavier, weighed down by the dense, precious metal of lived experience.

I left my 12th college life as one leaf a fierce, transformative storm. The landscape was forever altered. I carried the scars, the permanent knowledge that not everyone who shares your bread deserves a place at your table, that trust is a treasure to be guarded. But I also carried the jewels: the unwavering friendship that was my anchor, the ambitious, soul-deep love that was my compass, and the rediscovered, powerful voice that could turn trauma into comedy and silence into applause.

My hostel life was the crucible. It melted down the simple, lonely girl from the sun-dappled, quiet colony. In its unbearable heat, it burned away naivety. Still, in the cooling, it began to forge the core of someone new: stronger for having been broken, wiser for having been fooled, more compassionate for having tasted despair. I walked away not just with a marksheet, but with a doctorate in the intricate, painful, and beautiful science of human nature. My heart was no longer a simple, fragile thing. It was a mosaic, a lovely, complex picture pieced together from shards of betrayal, fragments of laughter, tiles of tender care, and the solid, golden pieces of triumph. Each crack was filled with the gold of resilience, a testament to the Japanese art of *kintsugi*, making the broken places not just strong, but more beautiful for having been broken. I had lived. I had felt. I had been brought to my knees. And I had risen, not just to my feet, but onto a stage, into a future I was now strong enough to face.

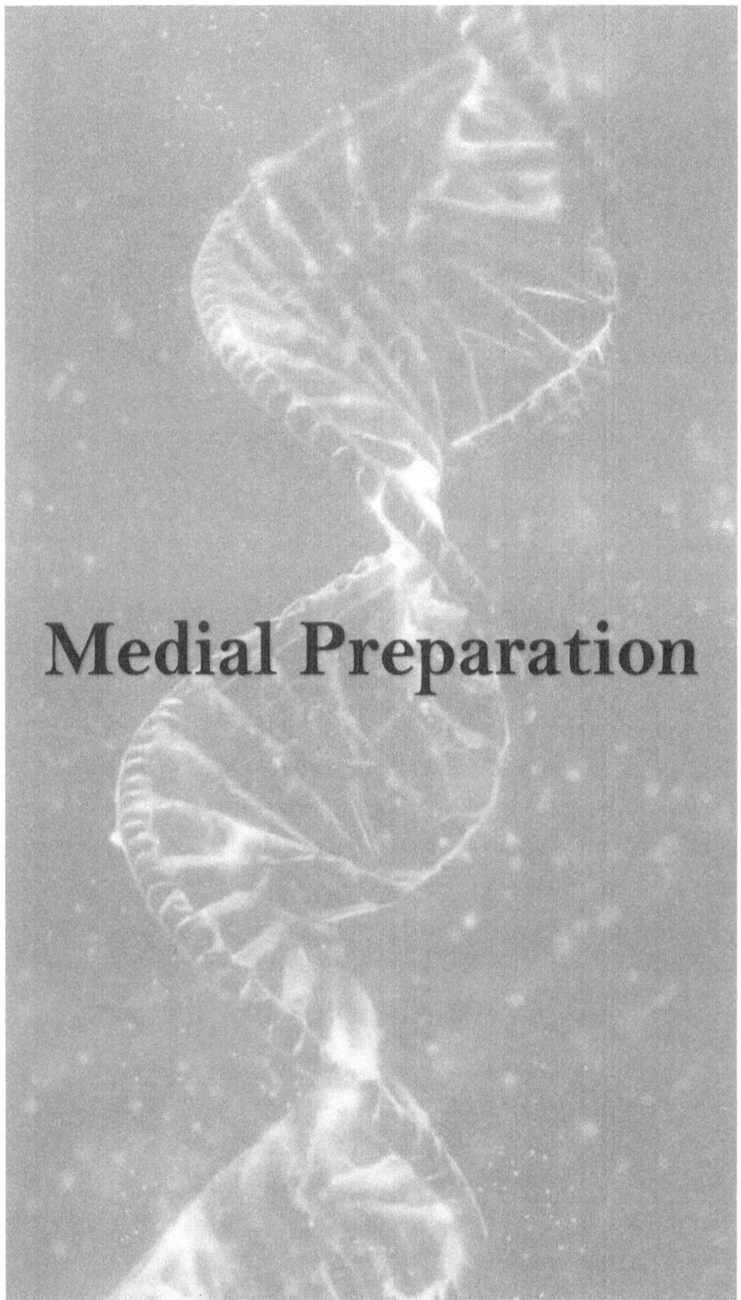

Medial Preparation

"We do not decide on our dreams; they decide for us. The only thing we have to do is determine how faithfully we'll adhere to them and at what price."

The memories of my medical training aren't just a chapter of research. It is a sweeping landscape of the soul, drenched in the monotone of exhaustion and the dazzling shining gold of a single fixed star. My room on the final day was not just a bedroom but an unspoken, sacred space. The walls were not covered with pictures of actors or pop stars; they were covered with anatomical charts of the human body, which were transformed into an outline of the tributaries and mountains I had to overcome. The kidney's cross-section seemed more recognisable to me than the veins on my palm. The smell was that of old papers, highlighter ink, and the midnight oil, which had evaporated into a lasting scent throughout the room.

My days weren't measured by hours, but rather by chapters completed, with solutions to problems and the gradual, painful loss of my doubts. I would wake up working at my desk, the cold morning lighting a pale witness to my daily routines. I would repeat all the movements that comprise the Krebs cycle as an incantation as I traced the pathways of the cranial nerves using an uneasy finger, shivering from the sleep deprivation. Physics was a world of unending logic, and chemistry was a dance of elements that I needed to dance in my brain. I became a researcher of shadows, observing them stretch and recede across my textbooks, signalling the end of another day sacrificed to a single goal.

The battle was a silent and constant partner. It was the pain in my eyes after 12 hours of looking at tiny print. It was the hollow sensation in my stomach, which was not necessarily hunger, but rather the pain of anxiety. It was the social gatherings that I resisted, the conversations I muttered, and the self-image I put off. I promised her, "Soon. After passing the test, you will be able to live your life again." My life shrinks to the size of the desk I was working at; I am transformed into an individual candidate, a vessel to be filled with information, and a mind that needs sharpening to become an arsenal for a single important day.

The pressure was not a force external to me but one that had been within me, embedded in the fabric of my soul. It was the unspoken desire in my father's eyes as the time came for him to bring me a teacup at 2 am. It was how my mother would walk through the house, as if the sound of her voice could break my concentration. It was the burden that hung over generations of historical stories, where it was more than a formality; it was an expression of family triumph, as well as the security and respect that were earned. I carried that weight on my sagging shoulders and in the tight girth of my spine as I scooted on my notebooks.

Then, the day arrived. The medical entrance exam room was a place of collective tension. The sound of the exam paper sounded like the reversal of a decision. I still remember my own breath, which was loud in my ears, as well as the racing, frantic beat of my heart when I was facing the examination. It was a bloody and beautiful battle. Every question was a battleground. Some I fought with quick, precise writing strokes, some I was encircled, marking them with logical thinking and a few scraps of my memory. I struggled to win every point, each percentage point, in a desperate way that was utterly terrifying and pure. It was the culmination. This was it. The sunrises and nights of silence, as well as all the different versions of me I hid in my textbooks.

As the Odisha JEE results arrived, they were not like numbers on a monitor. They were like the result of a decision. **3280 ranks in the general category.** In the grand rough hierarchy of dreams, it was a cliff. It was not the majestic high point I had imagined in my dreams; however, it was an esplanade. A narrow, unstable platform that I could look out over two different scenarios.

One route created by this rank led me to dental treatment. The letter of offer arrived with a heavy weight on my fingers. It was a key to the healing world I'd always wanted, but with another door. I studied it, this science of smiling. I discovered its precision, the blend of medicine and art, and its influence on one's health and confidence. I could imagine the benefits of living there: a fulfilling, meaningful life. I'd dress in an outfit, maybe not the white long coat of a doctor, however, but a neat, modern, clinical one. I would carry instruments, relieve pain, and create order from decay in the teeth. It was a sturdy and reputable path for birds in the hands.

Another invitation came through unexpectedly and was intriguing: Veterinary Science. It was an unexpected invitation to a harsh forest, not an urban zone. I imagined myself assisting animals with soft smiles and wide eyes to heal through a language that transcends words. This language was a call to an unmistakable, peaceful part of my being, a part seeking comfort in the simple pleasures of companionship, the basic animal simplicity. It was a world of mud, miracles, and awe of fur and stethoscopes. In a brief, stunning time, I let myself wander along that path in my head, surrounded by patients mewing and barking under the clear skies.

However, in the background, other siren calls, a third one was beginning to ring. It was the sound of engineering. It was always there; through a parallel path I had seen in my research: the beautiful mathematical certainty as well as the poetic and grounded nature of Physics. While biology described life's gorgeous chaos, physics talked about the immutable nature of the universe. Engineering was not designed to heal the body but to create universes. To invent to solve problems, to build mechanisms and structures that would improve society. It was a time of steel and silicon and code, of calculus and code and extending towards the infinitely creative.

I was at the most defining crossing point of my life. Three distinct scenes were emerging ahead of me. They were the exact dental clinic, the earthy vet's office, and the engineer's thriving workstation. The air was simultaneously suffused with the smells of antiseptic, Ozone, and hay from circuit boards.

"At crossing points, it is not enough to just pick a path. You decide who you'll become when you get there."

The decision was difficult. It wasn't a spreadsheet calculation of cons and pros. This was an excavation of the self. What was I underneath the layers of expectations? Did I really become the person I always believed I was meant to be? Perhaps I was an architect? Does my need to heal manifest in a medical environment, or could it be fulfilled by creating a bridge to connect isolated communities, constructing safe water systems to ward off illness, or developing technology that could save lives on a larger scale?

I was thinking about my family's financial records. The cost of private medical school was an immense amount of debt that my parents would gladly, quietly, carry. Vet schools, too, were not without their costs. Engineering, especially if you had an outstanding grade, gave an easier and often more economical path to stability. It also allowed me to ease the financial burden and not add to it. It was not a shrewd calculation, but rather acts of affection, and a duty that was now the basis of my dream.

The final decision to leave the dental chair and the option of pursuing veterinary medicine weren't rejections or denials of these noble choices. The decision was made in a deliberate, heartbreaking choice to seek an alternative to my ideal. I did not choose engineering as an escape route, but to reorient myself to my goals. I wanted to treat, but with prevention. I would be concerned for myself, but not through the process of creation. I'd put on the hard hat that goes over my white coat and my stethoscope, and I'd be listening to the beat of the machines that fuelled our modern lives.

This decision was met with astonished silence from a few and thoughtful smiles from others. However, for the first time that the results had been delivered, that knot in my chest started to ease. I wasn't abdicating my goal; I was **moving** it. I was taking the same drive to improve and help others to be a part of the solution, and putting it into an entirely different place. I was considering the future's features, its scope and ingenuity, its potential to have a broad impact, and the fact that the hands of my fingers, which were trained to solve problems using notebooks, would eventually be able to solve problems in the real, huge, awaiting world.

THE FOUNDATIONS OF A NEW WORLD

"Resilience isn't developed in the moment that you are safe from falling; however, it is born in the quiet, long excavation of your own body that begins when you fall onto the concrete."

The moment I left the tangible benefits of the dental chair I had obtained, the path to veterinary medicine beckoned, and it felt like stepping off a solid, well-marked track and into an uncharted, dense fog. The choice to pursue engineering was based on an intellectual conviction; however, in my heart, it felt initially like a space. The persona for "future doctor," the shell that I have inhabited for so many years, was shattered, while the one I was now, "future engineer," was hollow, like a costume that wasn't quite right.

The beginning days at Engineering College were a test of cognitive dissonance. The air did not smell of antiseptic, but of chalk and iron soldering. The language evolved from Greek and Latin terms to the savage beauty of C++ and the unstoppable mathematical logic of calculus. My colleagues talked of forces, not fevers; of algorithms, not antibodies. I felt like an unreachable ghost from a faraway country, snoring in the lecture halls, where my sorrow for the life I had imagined was an unspoken, invisible partner.

The battle this time was distinct. It wasn't the long race of all-consuming medical preparation. It was a struggle for **relevancy**. Did my brain, so well-tuned to master the intricacies that the liver is made of, change its wiring to comprehend the intricate workings of a microprocessor? Can the fervour that fuelled my late-night readings in biology transfer to the thermodynamics course? Shadows of the medical position, which was **3280**, did not appear as failure, but instead as a question that remained in my mind: *Did I choose the right path?*

I plunged myself into the new curriculum with a ferocious, perhaps reckless, enthusiasm. It was a way of putting aside doubt. If I could master this, my choice would be confirmed. In the evenings, I was not in a quiet space or in a noisy computer lab; the blue light of the screen was a new kind of night sun. My fingers, that had previously drawn diagrams of the heart, were now wired sloppily to breadboards. It was the "Eureka!" moments that came not from figuring out the path of the disease, but from watching an element of code I'd written eventually work perfectly, or from watching the bridge model I had calculated withstand every obstacle.

Then, slowly, and without warning, the shift started. It wasn't a flashing spark; it was a dawning light leaking into a dark space. I began to recognise that there was **humanity** in the machine. Making a user-friendly interface wasn't simply about programming; it's about understanding empathy and knowing how people interact with technology. Sustainable design of a structure was about the community, about caring for the environment. The engineering stale logic was exposed to its pulsating centre: It was to serve people.

The mentor of my medical school days has said, "Success is about persevering to discover your purpose." I thought my job was like being in an operating room or sitting in a dentist's chair. Engineering has taught me that my purpose is to resolve problems, build, and enhance. The canvas was changed; however, the desire to make order out of chaos, to fix the broken pieces, was fundamentally the same.

The cinematic theme of this chapter was not the high-energy, close-up action of the exam room, but rather a longer, slower panorama of a changing landscape. The soundtrack shifted from a straightforward, slow, tense piece to one featuring a layer of building synthesisers that sounded rhythmic, adding depth and creativity. There were videos of me and newly formed companions in arms laughing at a failed prototype, rejoicing over an event that was a success, our faces lit by the glow of a computer monitor showing a game we had built together. It was a different type of friendship, not forged through silent struggle, but through noisy, collaborative creation.

There were moments of profound echo. While studying biomechanics, I realised that our body is one of the most fantastic engineering marvels. When I was working on software for medical imaging in a research project, I could feel the two parts of my life, the discarded medical aspiration and the fully embraced engineering reality, meld to form a complete, satisfying whole. I wasn't merely an engineer. My experience was as an engineer with an ophthalmologist's perspective, which made my perspective distinctive.

"We create our futures not out of the blueprints we created for our initial plans, but rather from the enduring substances we find within the wreckage from our dreams."

The decision to choose engineering for its "future aspects" was no longer merely about jobs and financial security. The future was all about me. It was about creating the kind of person who could adapt, think in systems, and bring about tangible change through her thoughts and hands. The white coat symbolised the role of a specific person. The hard hat, as well as the laptop that coded, represented agency, as the authority to define the position itself.

As I look back from the beginning of the new world, I view the crossroads as a point where I am lost, but rather as an opportunity to forge. The sting of dismay, the pressure of making that unattainable decision, made me someone more powerful and refined. I brought the discipline of my medical training into my engineering work. I carried the compassion of my potential healer into my designs for technology. The compassion of a veterinarian for living beings influenced my fascination with ethics-based AI and sustainable technology.

I had made my way to the altar for aspiration and made a glaring offering. I had left with the tools. The desire didn't end; it **developed**. It evolved from a single place, a stethoscope on a chest, to a vast interconnected system, much like the circuit board that is lit up, with each connection being a source of a problem that I was able to help solve, a world I could influence in a different, yet not less profound, manner.

The story wasn't about becoming an erudite doctor. It was about transforming into. In the noisy, exciting, tense engineering world, amid the whirring servers and the sketch of a schematic, I felt the distinct, assured sound of my own becoming. It was the sound of a well-constructed machine with the perfect, silent operation of code. It was the peaceful, constant beat of a soul at peace, and finally creating the future it was intended to.

Engineering Days

A JOURNEY THROUGH DREAMS AND DARKNESS

My life, at the first significant moment of my life, was less an option and more of a tender, heartbreaking removal. I was a plant, carefully cultivated for the fertile, nourishing ground of the medical field. My soul was awed by the poetic nature of biology, the intricate dance of cells, as well as the stories written in blood and bone, and the enthralling mystery of the heart beating. Zoology was more than an area of study; it was my first language. The act of reading a book meant to sit and listen to a concerto; the process of dissecting an illustration meant sketching my beloved home country.

Perhaps fate, or the circumstances of life, provided a new trowel. The gate to the lush, green oasis of medicine was closed, and in front of me was an unlocked doorway to a completely different world: a highly regarded government engineering college. The opportunity sparkled with respect from society and a practical, gold-plated ticket that was admired by many. My parents, who were always there for me, let the decision fall into my shaking hands. It was my choice. It wasn't forced, but shaped by the quiet determination of a teen who saw the path to success as unending. The heart of my body, the naive romantic organ, screamed the most painful reality: "Let it go. Stop taking medicine forever." It was like an amputation of a potential self.

And I stepped over the threshold to enter the bleak, sharp, angular realm of engineering. I was an IT student who was as unfit as a garment three sizes too big. My computer knowledge was the equivalent of a kid's playtime, and it was that. I walked in with no hope but a desperate determination to make it through. My dream to become a doctor continued to haunt me, always a melancholy, constant partner. I would glance at the leaf and imagine the process of photosynthesis, listen to the beat of a heart, and imagine cardiology. My new acquaintances often spoke a different language. I was a refugee within my own world.

In this deportation, a small hope was ignited. It was a decent college. It was a *federal* college. It was a foundation, though it wasn't what I dreamed of. I told myself, "God will give you everything you desire, perhaps in indirect ways." Maybe this was the indirect route. I needed to believe it. I thought this battle would make me the person I was supposed to be. A strong and persevering person. I learned to smile at my heart, even having to teach my muscles how to do it from the beginning.

It was a sensory, emotional rollercoaster. I arrived at my hostel after dark, with the sun already sinking below the stark college buildings. The aunt I had was my saviour in the chaos, helping me organise my life in a small, shared space. Two roommates had already settled into an orderly scene. One of the roommates, P, was from a town close to mine. This simple connection between them was like a lifeline over a turbulent sea. In the moment of vulnerability, the promise was made to be sisters and open, and we could go home together. She was in Computer Science. I met a teacher who was an instructor through the eerie terrain of code.

In the beginning, the hostel served as a place to make new friendships. We formed a group of seven, a lively, social circle in which I was the only "IT" model from the 6 "CSE" tops. The place we gathered was a room shared by friends, where we shared snacks, conversations, and hopes. In the room, I heard my voice. I was a courtroom judge on biology, and my eyes would light up when I spoke about the evolution of animal behaviour. For a few hours, I wasn't just the lost medical student. I told stories and was an ardent. They watched me, sometimes amused, and sometimes fascinated. At those times, the ghost was still.

However, the ghost is never absent. A simple, sarcastic statement from someone else as a "friend", "Oh, you're right, but you did not *have* medical care, didn't you?" could shatter the illusion. The words were tiny; however, their impact was huge. They were a reminder of my perceived inadequacy and a brand. I was able to laugh through it and take the lump in my throat. I grew adept at enduring the sarcasm, the subtle indignation disguised as worry. I was the senile one, the one who worried too much about a vision in the end, "over."

The first cracks in my new life did not come from these blatant insults from the outside, but from my own inexperienced attempts to manage the social pressures. There was discussion of boys, couples, and romances that seemed a bit tinny compared to my academic struggles. In an effort to evade the spotlight and ward off my own, I invented a lie. I created an imaginary love story about a gentle, quiet boy from my past, the one I wanted to be with. I considered it an excellent cover, a way to declare, "I'm distracted, leave me to myself." I didn't realise that a lie, once released, takes on a life of its own and assumes forms its creator never would have. The boy, as it proved, was the author of his own complex story. My story fell apart, leaving a trail of confusion and embarrassment. This was my first experience of the destructive force of inauthenticity, which caused a small crack in the foundation of who I wanted to be.

The most powerful quake began with the person I'd held on to as a roommate and sister, P. Our bond intensified rapidly. I assisted P with her chores. I shared my belongings and fought for her with a vengeance. When my roommates fought, I was the facilitator, my peacemaker in desperate need to keep our family together. As a mediator, I was inevitably neglecting the third roommate, an insignificant oversight that later blossomed into thorns.

My affection with P is my weakness. When I saw another of our group members talking rudely to her, a fire ignited in me. I confronted the girl, insisting that she be gentler. This was a gesture that showed loyalty to me, thought. However, loyalty, in the complex math of hostel politics, is a monetary value that can easily be diminished. The girl was at P, and what she told me was something I did not fully understand. What happened, however, was a significant shift. P became angry at me. He did not do it with quiet, icy coldness, but rather with an intense, unjustified anger that made me scream. We had a violent fight driven by my personal anxiety over a poor math test. The words she used, "You're so interfering, so desperate," cut deeper than any criticism of my academic blunders.

The incident occurred the night before our first-semester tests. I was stuck on a fundamental concept in a state of anxiety, and I asked P for assistance. She was familiar with the subject. She turned to me, with my notes shivering in my hands. She resisted. She said, coldly and flatly, "No, I'm working." In that instant, the woman I loved disappeared. The person with whom I gave my dinner, all my gossip, and also my safety, was watching me drown and pulled back the rope. It was such a clear, sharp object that it cut the emotional ties completely. I passed the test on my own; however, some part of me had developed calcification. I realised it is not true that all hearts are refuges; some are fortresses with small gates.

A Personalised quote: "I entered a garden intended for engineers with a biologist's heart. They tried to cut me into their form without knowing that my roots were dreaming of an alternative sun."

THE KINDLING OF A FIRESTORM & THE BIRTH OF A VOICE

The beginning of my semester represented the shattered ruins of my innocent hopes. The second semester was the deliberate, frightening building that was my purgatory. The split with P was not a war, but we lived together in the fragile environment of our space. My reality was beginning to shrink and change under a baffling new pressure. It started with a simple Facebook message.

The name of his character isn't essential. He was a character well-known for his charisma and the "brand" of being wealthy and unassuming. He was a member of P's branch. Every time I tried to log in to my account, I would see a "Hi" from him. I found it annoying, intrusive. Then I complained to P, who laughed at me. "He's harmless and just a show off. Talk to him, and he's beneficial." So, I replied, out of an obligation to society and a little interest.

Our conversations started utterly dull. Food at the cafeteria, lecture times, and complaints about professors. He then assumed another role: the honest critic. "You know that the boys think you're insane," he'd say, and then go on to describe how my enthusiasm for subjects that weren't engineering-related appeared to be a bit too exuberant. He suggested I be more controlled, more "cool." With my desperation to be accepted, I took his advice. He was my social guide, offering me a glimpse into the male perspective in the hostel. I felt incredibly grateful. He seemed thoughtful and eager to share the truth with me.

My group of girls scolded me. "Don't be near to him too much," they'd tell me, with faces covered in a fear I mistakenly took for a sense of possessiveness. "He's in trouble." But what kind of trouble can be found in impersonal chats on the internet? We have never spoken in person. We never exchanged glances across the cafeteria. Our bond was only in cyberspace. I dismissed their concerns. "We're only friends on social media," I'd insist, not realising that in the realm of public opinion, perception is the sole truth.

For me, one of his strengths was his writing. He had a blog called "My life My Way," where he wrote achingly beautiful pieces about people he liked from the college we attended or from his class. His writings were vibrant, filled with longing and poetic observations. I was genuinely impressed. It really inspired me. I'd always written journals filled with emotion and poems, but I was amazed when he demonstrated the advantages of blogging. He wasn't a competitor and was more of an inspiration. I started to consider using my own words.

I didn't anticipate the nuclear consequences of this distant literary connection. The girl he adored, we'll call her R, was an awe-inspiring queen bee who had an incredibly strong beehive. She had, as I later discovered, an ex-boyfriend outside of the university. She had resisted my online acquaintance. However, when whispers reached her that he regularly communicated with *me*, the IT girl's anger was ignited. Jealousy, maybe. Or territorial resentment. It's also the gruesome game of setting a goal.

The whispers began slowly, then turned into a shout, Lena as well as he. Lena is now his primary source of distraction. Lena is after him. Lena was... Lena is... got uglier, touching not only my actions but also my personality. My social media connections were turned into a shady, obsessive relationship. The hive was ablaze with violence. R and her comrades, an influential group, launched a campaign of subtle, insidious intimidation. They would mute when I was in a room, and then burst into laughter. They wrote unclear, sharp status updates. "Some people don't have self-esteem." "Knowing what you are worth is crucial."

My acquaintances, those whom I had advised earlier, were looking at me with disdain. It was sour, and the social price of defending me was too high. As one by one the gossips disappeared. I was unreliable. My explanation, "We simply talk about everyday things, he's a lover of another person!" sounded pathetic and desperate. It was like I was sucked into a tale that I had never composed.

In a panic, I did what was unimaginable. I sent a message to *him*, my online guide, who caused this catastrophe. "Please," I typed with trembling hands, "tell your friends, and tell R that there's nothing in common between us. They're spreading terrible things. Please, please clarify this." His reply was an ice bucket after my last flash to hope "You mad girl, take a break. Get rid of me."

The ground was gone under me. The person I considered to be a friend, and for whom I was now suffering social destruction, not only was unwilling to help, but instead pushed me further into the crack. The deceit was utterly unforgivable. Then the cyber-attacks grew. The Facebook profile I had was compromised. Innocuous, childish posts were created using my profile. The mobile, which was my final private area, felt snubbed. I was not able to prove it, but I was certain. The message was clear: We can connect with you anytime. You're nothing.

My second-semester exams were approaching, and I felt numb. I couldn't focus on my studies. Words on the paper became blurred into the imagined whispers of the corridor. My hope of getting my marks to switch my field to something else, *anything* else, was a distant memory. I was not successful, not only in academics, but also spiritually. When the results were announced, R posted her triumphant status on her Facebook page: **"First impressions are not always the final impression."** It was her triumphant lap. Her scheme to sever me from my family, to break me, had been a success.

In the wake of that, I was the shell of my former self. I became deaf and was in a state of silence. I stopped talking to everybody. My hostel became a swarm of foes. My roommates, in particular the unloved third, were now free to make snide remarks. I had no allies in my branch. I was totally by myself. The pain was constant, grieving for my medical dreams and the recurring nightmare of the assassination of a character. How do I explain this to my family? "I'm not doing well because the girl is jealous of a Facebook chat?" It sounded wild even to me.

In the total zero state, an entirely new form of life appeared. If the world silenced my voice around me, I'd shout into the darkness of the internet. I started a blog. Not the literary, inspiring one I thought of; instead, it was an unfinished bleeding archive of hurt. I composed poems. Anguished, savage poems about betrayal, lonely dreams, that felt like broken bones within the skin. I gave my suffering the name, a shape, and a rhythm. I also, in doing so, snatched a bit of its strength.

In parallel, I started an online group on Facebook**, "STOP CHILDLABOR"** The reason was a primal desire to seek the light. If my world were a dark one, I'd try to be a light to others, even if only in a symbolic way. I did research, I published articles, and turned my despair into advocacy for the weak. The two actions of writing about my suffering and pursuing some cause became the two foundations of my survival. The writing was my way of expressing myself, the act of activism was my penance, and my prayer. I was without a smile, along with my friends and my education. However, I discovered my voice and motivation in the ashes. They were tiny and fragile, and yet they were *my own*. Nobody could steal them, and no one could disperse false rumours about their motives. They were the very first stones of a new foundation laid in the darkest and darkest night.

"They called my name and turned me into a cage. I then took the syllables that they used to lock their doors and made them into keys. I dubbed the key "my pen."

THE FORGE & THE ANVIL: SCULPTING A FORTRESS

The third semester began with the stark vision of a survivor observing a battlefield. The battle over my status in the social world was over. My hope of changing my branch was a smouldering corpse on the field. The only way to go forward was through the rubble with the two relics I had rescued in my writing, as well as my infantile sense of the purpose of my life. I needed to come to terms with and accept the fact that I had earned an IT degree. It wasn't the punishment for a crime, and it was the barren ground I had to prepare to cultivate. The acceptance of this was not a surrender. It was a strategic redeployment.

My solitude was now an actual space, a room within the room. I was able to inhabit it fully. Social media ceased to function as an exercise and turned into an instrument as a library, a bridge to a world that was not my horrifying campus. I invested myself in my **"STOP Child Labour"** initiative. It gave me a guideline to answer, "What are you up to?" a question that was never asked before; however, I had to know the answer myself. It was because I was *engaged in* something.

Through this project, I met two of the founders of a growing social enterprise. Both were alums of the top IITs. They were working on something tangible that was aiding artisans. They required online votes for the grant contest. I mobilised my small, damaged network. I spent hours promoting them. They were friendly, grateful. In the very first moment in nearly one year, I felt *confident*. I sat in awe that my brain and heart were still productive. I longed for the mentorship that would guide me into a fulfilling career.

The light flash seemed to be too bright for the shadows that remained with me. The old poison was found in new veins. My online friend, the writer, the betrayer, was not finished. The message he sent, "I am going to ruin you," was not a naive threat. His network, which now appeared to include unexpected allies such as sure seniors and even some from my former gang, tried to denigrate the new project. Some whispers reached the IIT founders, subtle warnings about me being a "drama" and having an "unstable" nature. My efforts to construct a ladder from the pit were met with hands shaking the walls and releasing stones.

The most brutal cut was a result of my past that I considered sacred. My best friend from 12th grade college, a girl I adored as a real sister, who's verbal scoldings and physical shoving I had to endure, and later was forgiven for out of pure love and unwavering devotion, ended my life. There was no fight. No dramatic scene. It was a quiet, chilly silence. The social media interaction ended. She didn't return my calls. She was aware of something. Some kind of rumour or bizarre story about the engineering scandal was reported to her. Without a single query and without allowing me to tell my story, she sentenced me to a life of exile from our past. The loss I suffered was a different type of grief. It wasn't the stinging loss by P or the savage resentment of R. It was the gradual, cold death of a relationship I thought could not be destroyed. It made me realise that the person I thought was my "character" could be a mark that would spread throughout time and contaminate even the most innocent aspects of my life.

I learned the ultimate, most difficult lesson: in the business of survival, friendships are not all assets. Some are liabilities. Certain people are not acquaintances; they are auditors waiting for your failure so that they can shut down the account. I made a brutal decision. I broke any ties with male acquaintances, online or off. Every contact was a possibility of speculation or a weapon for the future. My social circle shrank to zero. I was a monastic scholar writing a scribe of tears. My blog grew in size, and my school notes became more detailed and precise. I swapped humanity's chaos connections for the quiet, calm silence.

This was a test in strict discipline. I was a ghost, speaking only when asked. I ate on my own. I sat in one of the library's quietest spaces. The noise of the hostel became an insignificant buzz. I had built a fortress with tall, robust walls. Inside, I felt secure. On the outside, I was able to hurt myself without being noticed and heal without being asked questions.

The inevitable reshuffling of hostel rooms marked the fifth semester. It was a brand-new nightmare. My roommates made it clear that I wasn't wanted. In the chaos of bureaucratic procedures, they were also afraid of being thrown in with a random stranger. They flitted between telling me to quit and begging me to stay, with their disdain and desire for me to stay at the forefront. In the evening before my shift began, they unleashed a torrent of abuse intended to sever the last bits of me. They slammed me with two major injuries: my failure in school ("You didn't even earn good grades after you left medical school"), along with my character ("Everyone knows what you're as"). I sat on my bed, pretending I was asleep, and letting the words take over me like a torrent of acid rain. Then, something odd took place. The acid stopped burning, but it did temper. My core became hard the night before.

The following day, I shifted my stuff in a detached, cold effectiveness. I occupied the middle berth that they did not need. I gave up trying to make them feel loved. I quit being the peacemaker. I became courteous, unmovable, and determined. My anxiety, which was their primary motivator, had gone. Instead, there was a calm, strong determination.

In this transformation, I discovered Cory Booker, then the Mayor of Newark, via social networks. His words were not just a recitation of a slogan and were calls to action. "Your life has to be a verb," the man said. "The world changes because of those who are present." His tales of service to the community, as well as his courage in facing huge problems with unwavering compassion and determination, resonated in my fortress. The man became my mentor in virtual form. His knowledge was the anvil on which my ferocious resolve was transformed into something practical. I wasn't just constructing walls; I was laying the foundation for a tool.

I started to defend myself, I began to fight back, not with screams, but with honesty. If I were criticised, I would present the facts with a calm, precise voice. I was taught to guard my energy with ferocity. Hackers attacked me on my mobile phone. The final attack was the final nail. If I didn't have a private space in which to express my grief to my family, I'd publish it publicly. My blog evolved into more than a poetry journal. It became a journal. I wrote about the injustices and bullying, as well as about perseverance. I have stopped hiding my story. *Do you want to tell me about yourself?* I thought. *Let me provide you with the complete, authentic words.* The act of writing the story down and owning it was the most potent form of restoration.

When I finished the fifth semester, I was no longer an opportunistic victim. I was a recollection of my own personal life and a planner for my future. The girl who was awed by friendship considered it a vulnerability. The woman who feared the rumours has now revealed the truth. It was a complete transformation. I had entered the forge with broken bones and emerged not hard, but tough. The fire had not destroyed me; it was what made me who I am today.

"They mistook my silence as a sign of defeat. It wasn't silence. It was the solitary concentration of a sculptor selecting which pieces from the stone to cut away until they reveal the figure."

THE CONSTELLATION ASCENDANT: FROM SURVIVAL TO SANCTUARY

The last act of my engineering story was an exercise in the bittersweet peace. The sixth-semester drama over the room shift culminated in a poetic retribution administered by the firm but fair host warden, who said, "Ma'am." Exhausted from the squabble, I had made an official request for an upgrade. As the allotment list was sent out, I was on my own in a three-bed apartment on the fifth floor of the junior block. My roommates from my previous time were put right next to me. The punishment they'd hoped to inflict on me, being exiled, was handed to all of us. My initial fear of being alone in a new building was quickly alleviated by a gentle junior who wished for my space. She was not often around, studying with her peers, and I was able to enjoy the privacy I had selected, not imposed. It was a refuge.

This batch was calmer. My chaotic block was on the floor below. There, in the middle of strangers with no connection to my stories, I was able to breathe. I concentrated with a laser-like intensity on my final project of the year, GATE examination preparations for an M.Tech, and an undiscovered, growing interest, I'd cultivated through documentaries and writing about astrophysics. The Universe, with its immense, silent complexity, attracted me, who had always loved biology. It was a brand-new idea, not a child's imagination, but an adult mind seeking deep order.

My project was the Rubicon. When I realised that no one from my group would join with me, the feeling of being alone hurt, but also liberated me. I picked a subject I was really interested in, not one designed to impress. My project's guide, who was a senior faculty member and HOD, was a strict woman whom I initially feared. She, however, was able to spot my singular dedication. Instead of ignoring me, she gave me precise, valuable advice. She admired my effort. In her, I discovered an unexpected academic friend, a professional who judged me based on what I did, but not on my previous experiences.

Then, it was Lakshmi. The hotel's cleaning lady was to clean our floors. She was in her 50s, struggling with diabetes, with her hands rough from her work. Her smile faded, but it was warm. We had a chat during a time when I was clearly ill. She offered me a cup of ginger tea from her home. It was a gesture of kindness amid a sea of disinterest. The bond was formed, unspoken and profound. She would cook me homemade food at times, or assist me with errands if I was lost in books. When I wanted to make a payment, she would not, but she'd decline, gently patting my cheek. "You're like a child who's away from her home," she'd say in the local dialect. Through her, I saw the simple, uncomplicated motherly love I longed for. I was her advocate whenever snobbish peers complained about her job. Our friendship was the most authentic I developed in the institution, unaffected by competition, status, or gossip. It was a bond of human compassion. She was my refuge and a constant reminder that the qualities of love and dignity are found in the humblest of hearts.

The seventh and 8th semesters were not without a bit of friction. The junior in my room also had a companion who moved into the block and would frequently talk loudly in front of my door, which was a serious distraction during my exam preparations. However, my resiliency was now an exercised muscle. I purchased a pair of high-quality headphones. I began to practice meditation. The sound of their voices was an irritation but not a cause for concern. The fortress I'd constructed had comfy furniture and windows looking out towards my future.

Then, the Universe sent a signal. A form I'd nearly forgotten for a workshop with a visiting student at ARIES, a renowned institute for astronomy and astrophysics, came in with a letter of acceptance. My heart was euphoric. It was a confirmation by the Universe itself. It was a way, even if it was a narrow one, to my next dream. I could see myself amid instruments and information, searching for the mysteries of the stars.

Then, the second shoe fell. My final semester grades were in. The only thing I could find, in the midst of passing marks, was one obvious "Back Paper" within one class. This was irony, a work of savage poetry. The astrophysics field was chosen, but was stymied by a single engineering paper. The old shame was beginning to be rekindled. My roommates' voices, "You didn't even earn good marks," repeated for a short time.

But I wasn't the girl from the second semester. I scanned the paper on the back and the ARIES letter in tandem. The first was a mishap on a path I was compelled to take, and the other was a way to get onto an avenue I chose. The two paths didn't stop me; they shaped my path. I used to clean the back sheet, a simple administrative task. However, the ARIES opportunity was a bright spot to follow.

As I walked out of the college gates for the last time, I felt no remorse for the school. But I was filled with admiration for the man it pushed me to be. I wasn't the optimistic biological enthusiast with a naive attitude who came in. It was my turn to be a journalist born in flames. A resolute person who learned to sustain herself within her own circle. A woman who knew the difference between genuine kindness and a performative friendship. I had a voice honed by the silence of oppression. I had a mission and discovered it through advocacy. I had witnessed the gloomiest human pettiness and the most radiant glimmer of pure humanity in people like Lakshmi, my guide for my project.

My engineering career wasn't a traditional success story. This was a survival tale. It was about an ominous seed that fell on cement rather than the soil, but instead of dying, it figured out how to break the stone with its roots. It was not there to search for the water but rather to show that it was able. The medical vision was not substituted; it was surpassed. My enthusiasm for science did not end; it grew beyond the microcosm of biology into the space-time macrocosm, and the complex computer code became an instrument, not the master.

I'd always wanted to laugh out of my soul. In the end, I did. It was a sombre, complex smile that held the memories of tears but was illuminated by the hard-earned glow of self-awareness. They'd tried to write me a story using the ink of the rumour. However, in the end, I took the pen. It was a matter of beginning to write.

PERSONALISED QUOTE & EPILOGUE:

"They were able to see a lonely woman who was sitting in the darkness. They weren't aware of how I learned the names of stars. My pain wasn't a space; It was the darkness that held my galaxies together. The crucial brightness that had made my personal glow, once I ignited it, was incomparable to ignore."

My story serves as a map to anyone who is lost in a place not of their own. There are no rumours about you. You are not the product of your mistakes. You are not reflected in the faces of people who do not understand your true self. You are the silent and unrelenting writer and the obstinate gardener in concrete and the astronomer of your personal soul. Locate your pencil. Find your cause. Locate your Lakshmi. Don't look at the stars. The road ahead is yours. The story is yours. The thrilling, complex, gorgeous conclusion is yours to create.

MBA Journey

THE FRACTURED BLUEPRINT

My life, which was once meticulously designed, is now in shards all around me. Each piece of glass represents a different version of a future that may never come to pass. My compass was set to only one point of light: the GATE test, an eminent IIT, a PhD in a foreign country, and a lifetime of reputable science. It was a simple equation, a rational development. I was able to solve for "X," and "X" was always a happy, prosperous life in the world. I even secured the position of a researcher at Stanford in bioinformatics, a notable achievement on my resume and a confirmation of my technical abilities. This was to be my first step into the future, a testament to my merit before I could reach my ultimate goal. The universe, as it turns out, has a mathematical system that is more complex than the one I was taught.

And then, it was clear that the base had shattered. The causes are intimate and massive, a result of personal turmoil and rapid, seismic shifts in the world, which made my carefully planned route disappear as if it were a figment of my imagination. The Stanford chance vanished in the mist in the midst of uncertainty around the world. Preparing for my GATE exam, fueled by numerous midnight oil, I encountered the wall of exhaustion so complete that it was a space. The dream I had conceived of that I had put up with so much did not just disappear; it vanished. The silence that followed was deafening. The silence was an untrue result of a complicated calculation that just gave an error. I had lost not only a strategy but also my entire identity tied to it. Who was I if I wasn't the upcoming doctor? Sharma, the scientist?

In the echoes of that loss, I lost myself. It was a hazard to live the "easy living", the dull screen and the void of social media did not provide any comfort, just the feeling that I was lost. I was ghostly in my own existence, engulfed by the ghost of the person

I had hoped to be. The desire that once blazed like a pure blue flame had sputtered out, leaving just an ashy residue and the throbbing of an unending hurt: *What now?*

It was during this winter of spirit that whispers, not shouts, first appeared. A whisper of peace. It's about cleansing, not just a resume, but a soul. The rational mind rebelled. An MBA wasn't part of the equation. What was an MBA at a school known for its meditation and spirituality? It seemed like a contradiction and a departure from the rigorous, prestigious course I was taking. When you're looking around the ruin of your own design, you start to notice different types of materials. It's not just concrete and steel, but also air and light.

My move into Sri Sri University was not an academic shift. It was an urgent pilgrimage. I did not arrive with the enthusiasm of a top performer and with the peaceful need to escape the expectations I had set for myself. The campus, a sanctuary of lush greenery and utter calm, was entirely at odds with my engineering inclinations. The air was not swaying to the sound of machinery, but seemed to be enveloped in silence. Here, I made an unspoken, personal vow and a mantra that was my mantra during the beginning of my journey: ***"I came here not to create a new career and to build an identity. I will make use of the silence to hear an inner voice that I've lost myself."***

The whole-life rhythm here was a shock for my weakened system. My previous life was filled with imperative, linear tasks. The day here was circling. It began not with any problem sets, but with a moment of meditation. As I sat in the peaceful gardens in the early morning, guided by my mentors, whose calm seemed invincible, I faced the chaos within. The first few sessions were painful. My mind, like a server array of worries and failed plans that would not go away. However, slowly, and inexplicably, the quietness of the outside began to creep in. It didn't eliminate it; however, it created an area within it. In the space, I saw my dreams shattered without being cut by them.

The lectures were another type of insight. In my world of engineering, knowledge was absolute and binary. In a class on ethics in leadership, the professor was asked, "How do you be a good leader in a society that encourages those who do not?" The question hung in the air, not as a matter to be resolved, but as a mirror to be held. The discussion that followed was complex, messy, and human. It was the first time in my life that I was not learning how to alter external systems; instead, I was learning to examine my own inner systems, my beliefs, and my scars, as well as my resilience. The class was buzzing not only with intellectual enthusiasm but also with a collective quest for meaning.

I was initially resistant to this change. My previous self was the rigorous engineer. laughed at this "softness." However, an inner, tired portion of me was thirsty for it. The tapestry-weaving strategy, which included religious fervour, case studies, and mindful breathing, felt less like a course and more like a thoughtful, ongoing act of healing. I wasn't simply absorbing knowledge; I was also learning to breathe and to live in the moment, without being weighed down by a future that was sadly gone.

This was the unfiltered and unadulterated beginning of my MBA journey. It did not begin from the desire to succeed, but rather out of surrender. I had given up my idea of an engineering lab in MIT for a mat to meditate on in Odisha. In the process, although I was unaware of it, I was embarking on my first engineering project by rebuilding an entire living space from the inside out.

THE ALCHEMY OF BROTHERHOOD AND BELONGING

In the beginning, my journey was one of solitude and reflection; the universe, in its wisdom and gentleness, provided me with the perfect mirror I needed: my brothers. The "Brotherhood in Diverseness" wasn't a university slogan, but rather the real, living, sometimes vibrant and delicious real-world experience that showed me how a new self can connect to the world that it had left behind.

The warmth of the sun, real and warm, started to shed the cold internal glare of my failings. I walked around the campus, not as an uninvolved spectator but as a hesitant participant in the symphony of various languages, the rounded vowels of Tamil, and the lyrical cadence of Marathi. The quickfire Hindi became no longer a noise; it was a song I gradually learned to appreciate. My first interaction with a person was in a group project. I was there, my North Indian engineer with a broken dream, joined by an energetic Marathi commerce graduate and an extremely meticulous South Indian computer scientist. My timid "Namaskar" was met not with corrections but with enthusiastic, uplifting words. Their laughter became an opportunity to bridge the gap rather than a barrier. In their eye, I wasn't the one who wasn't able to get to IIT. It was simply a new acquaintance who was having trouble with my pronunciation. The simple, unearned recognition was a saviour I had not realised I needed.

My brothers became them. It wasn't in a casual family sense, but in an established, logical manner. We went through the rigorous requirements of the MBA, not as a team of competitors or a group. The lab we used was the dining room table. There, the most profound lessons in management were served alongside

Puran Poli and Sambar. Food was the first language we spoke in mixing. I told stories about my childhood home and the pressure-cooker expectations that had defined my identity while we ate bowls of daal. They told their stories of family-owned companies, of temples in the South of monsoons in the coastal region. Our dining table was our boardroom, in which we argued about the market's dynamics and emotions with the same enthusiasm.

An evening of starlight, following a tough day, a sigh of silence passed over us. It was a peaceful silence, born of confidence. And in that silence, my own truth, which I had been avoiding for so long, finally came out. "I am here as I've lost everything that I thought I had," I admitted with my voice barely higher than an ebb. "I arrived at this place... damaged. To be at peace, or to end the roar." I sat in fear for the sake of pity, or for awkwardness. But instead, I noticed an incredibly resonant. It was as if the Marathi brother spoke about the family pressure to buy a company that he did not love. He also shared that his South Indian friend shared his personal struggle with anxiety, which was masked by his academic excellence. In the moment of vulnerability, the bond between us grew stronger. We weren't MBA students. We were pilgrims with a secret burden, each seeking an easier way to travel.

Our diverse backgrounds, which I may consider a challenge, were actually our most significant strategic advantage. In tackling a case study, we would approach it from different angles, shaped by our diverse worldviews: my analytical engineering mind, his systems-thinking mindset, his pragmatic, grounded Marathi viewpoint, and his precise, process-centric South Indian approach. We were taught about constructive conflicts and about disagreeing without causing discord. A heated debate about the best marketing approach would eventually end in laughter over an evening meal, and the disagreement would be absorbed into the greater structure of our respect.

This brotherhood was the concrete implementation of peace that I learned through meditation. The peace within me enabled me to really listen to them. Their acceptance and trust gave me the security to test my emerging self, who wasn't just a result of grades and big plans. I discovered that leadership doesn't only involve giving direction from the front, but also about having the courage to show vulnerability within an open group of people who trust each other. It's about creating a place where people from Marathi or South Indian backgrounds, and a heartbroken engineer, can openly share their fears and, in doing so, discover the strength of their community.

"We arrived as fragments of puzzle pieces," I later wrote in my notebook. "Through the magic of shared meals and a silent exchange, we realised that we were not fragments in the first place; we were one complete image waiting to be put together. Our differences weren't borders that separated us. They were the lines that gave our family its distinctive, beautiful form."

It was the MBA from Sri Sri University. In the end, I received two degrees that are inseparable. The first was the discipline of management, a framework for comprehending the world. The second, more valuable, was how to create human connections to learn my own place within them. I was there to purify my soul by sitting in silence. I was able to graduate after discovering that the soul can also be cleansed and incredibly strengthened by the raucous, joyful, sweet, and extremely caring community that is not based on similarities but instead on the incredible, enduring variety of our human journey. The peace I felt was not the quiet of solitude. It was the peaceful sound of belonging.

The Bangalore
Experience

It is not just the record of events; it is the skeleton of a change. It tells the tale of a soul that came to Bangalore carrying a master's and an elusive dream, and returned with a new self-forged by the endless, beautiful heat at the heart of Bangalore. These pages are my testimony to the adversity that teaches the lessons of loneliness, the bonds that unite, and the dreams that only a city such as Bangalore can smash and then resurrect. Take a close look; you could feel your heart beating in these words.

"A city doesn't need to verify your proof of identity. It wants your determination. In return, it will tell you an account."

THE FIRST GULP OF AIR – ARRIVAL AND THE ABYSS

The train let out a long metallic sigh as it sped into Bangalore City Junction station, enveloping me in its scorching, raucous embrace. I was there, an unprotected relic of contradictions, carrying my MBA degree from Sri Sri University, a hard-to-read document in my hands, and my heart racing in the midst of no protection. The air seemed filled with a potent cocktail of jasmine, diesel, burning oil, and undiluted, pure possibility. This was an experience of sensory explosion. After the tranquillity of the university, where ambition was quiet in the library nooks, Bangalore was a roaring rock concert. Auto-rickshaws whizzed around like maniac beetles with their horns creating an urgent symphony. The cries of vendors made a splash through the crowd, selling everything from idles with steam to smartphone covers. Many lives streamed by me; each is a story of its own, etched with intention and stress, or even a tired sense of optimism.

This was the scenario I decided to accept. The professional, predictable job proposal from the NOIDA corporate house was an unrealized message in my inbox. I had to decline it. For many people, it was a sign of insanity. "A bird that was in your hands," the well-meaning uncle warned me the voice of his uncle, his voice crackling across the line. My hand was empty, as if it held another person's dreams. Revenue charts and sales targets seemed like a language my soul could not comprehend. I needed a dictionary of its meanings, not just a list of numbers. Bangalore, with its infamous chaos, was the perfect place to create it.

My first house was a guesthouse I paid for in Koramangala, so small that the walls felt like they were eavesdropping on my conversations. The hunt for it was an unintentional baptism of fire, rushing through the listings which promised "sun-lit rooms" that were, in reality, cabinets, and landlords who looked at one woman with a mixture of lust and suspicion. When I finally opened the door of my little kingdom, a swell of happiness fell over me. It was so strong that it almost knocked me off my feet. This was my first chance to earn silence. The city's sound was alive and filtered through the window, serving as a constant reminder that I was an active participant, not just an observer.

The job search started with a clean, optimistic spreadsheet. I'd dress in my most formal clothes and wear the look with confidence. I would walk through the glamorous glass atriums in tech parks in Electronic City and along the outer ring roads. Interviews were a unique type of theatre. "Tell me a little about your life," they'd ask, and I'd perform my rehearsal monologue as if I were an imposter trying to audition for a role dubbed "Professional." A question like, "Where do you see yourself in five years?" would hang in the cool air. I'd look back with my voice screaming, "Alive! I want to feel alive.

Rejections were sent in friendly or automated messages. "We regret to let you know." ..." Each one was like a bit of death as it confirmed the nagging doubt that had been following me at the railway station. I would return to my small bedroom, remove the dress, and lie down on the bed, observing the ceiling fan cut through the gloomy afternoon light. The gap between dream and reality has never been so stark as an actual gap. I was missing the friendly friendships of the university and the certainty of a routine. Time was an unfathomable, frightening thing that I had to design on my own.

But Bangalore, in its ever-changing duality, was a city that offered consolation in exchange for rewards. When I was tired on weekends from the demands of spreadsheets, I'd head out to the park for a walk. I stumbled upon the tranquil old-fashioned twilight of Cubbon Park in which the city's roar diminished to a whisper. I sat under the shade of massive rain trees, my back against their thick bark, and took a deep breath. I came across Ranga Shankara as I sat for the evening, captivated by a Kannada piece I didn't comprehend, but felt within my bones. In the bustling food stalls in VV Puram, I'd indulge in a delicious masala dosa, with its fresh texture and spicy chutney, which was a short-term balm for my wounded spirit. The city was teaching me a vital lesson: Resilience isn't just built through the pursuit of the goal, but rather when you are at peace with yourself in the middle of the quest.

A few days ago, following a tough interview during which I had a slip of the tongue in a report, I was walking back, my phone in hand for directions. While walking along a busy footpath, an unexpected, nauseating sensation of lightness slid into my pocket. My phone, my map, my contact list, and my fragile connection to the world vanished. A cold, icy panic gripped me. I turned round; however, the ocean of faces that were indifferent only mirrors my own aching despair. I was drifting.

A gentle tapping upon my shoulder. A senile man with a face full of wrinkles and gentle lines pulled my cell phone. His eyes, gentle and crinkled around the edges, were looking at mine. " *Idu nimdu,*" the man whispered gently in Kannada. You have it. He handed it to me in a stupefied hand, gave me a subtle, sly nod, and disappeared to his crowd. He left before I could say a simple thank you.

I was there, holding the device that was retrieved, and my eyes were tearing up. The phone wasn't the only thing I was having trouble with. It was a line of connection and a message sent from the city itself. There's no need to be alone. You're not the only one in this. We're all looking out for one another in this area. The gesture of kindness, which was not intended for me, made me feel safe. It was the feeling I needed to remind myself that, beneath the shiny exterior, Bangalore had a heartbeat and an inner conscience. I returned to my home that evening with no regrets of an unsuccessful interview but filled with joy from an enthralled faith. The hunt would continue, but I'd not be an outsider in the search process.

THE AXIS POINT – FINDING FOOTING IN THE FRENZY

The phone call from Axis Bank came on a Thursday. Its HR voice was clear, professional, and to me it sounded like a choir of angels. The process of interviewing was a tangle of intense discussions that felt more like a long conversation than an interview. They questioned about market trends; however, they also inquired about pressure. "Tell us about the time you made a mistake," one panellist said, her eyes fixed. For the first time in my life, I didn't give a textbook-like, sanitised answer. I spoke about the NOIDA invitation I'd turned down, the confusion that it caused, and the shaky conviction that led me. I spoke from my heart, not my resume. It was a frightening risk. It was also a crucial turning point in my life.

The offer letter arrived in my mailbox, and I didn't cry or leap. I sat down in the quiet in my PG room. I placed my hands flat on the laptop's cool screen and exhaled the breath I knew I'd held for months. I had done it. I had turned an emotion, a ferocious pull in my soul, into a concrete beginning.

The moment I walked into the Axis Bank office on my first day was like walking into the bridge of a spaceship. The clean glass, the quiet but powerful energy, the ferocious steps of the employees. It was a far cry from the smoky, philosophical halls of my university. My desk was a small piece of territory that was claimed. The first weeks were full of terms, processes, and an arduous, never-ending learning curve. Deadlines were not a matter of choice. They were the unchangeable laws of physical science. The company's rhythm was constant, a stark contrast to the semester-bound pace of the academic world.

It was at this point that I got to know the people I call my "idiot buddies." The phrase that was born out of our self-deprecating humour was our most flattering praise. There was Arjun, always hungry programmer of Kerala with a smile that was able to ease any tense moment; Priya, the fiercely fashionable Tamilian marketing expert who was able to locate the ideal Irani cafe in the early hours of 1 AM and Rohan who was one of the Bengali Finance analysts that carried a collection of poetry in his purse along with the financial statements. We were the orphans of aspiration and were being thrown into the same fiery furnace.

They were my Bangalore. After a long day and nights, we'd gather in a part of a noisy restaurant in Indiranagar or eat a heap of biryani at a nearby dhaba. Our conversations ranged from workplace gossip and shared worries about rent costs to big plans and totally absurd jokes. Priya would analyse my unsuccessful dating efforts using the exactitude of an audit for a campaign. Arjun would make us take on the most bizarre street food contests. Rohan would then suddenly recite the words of Tagore under the yellow light of a streetlight. This made the street's chaos feel intense. With them, the city's heaviness did not disappear, but it was manageable, and even humorous. They were the human skeleton of my new world as evidence that I was building more than a business; I was creating an entire world.

The work itself started to transform from a series of chores into an image. I was able to master solving complex client issues and locating the personal story hidden within the information. There was satisfaction in ending a loop and contributing to a team's win. The professional image that I'd been searching for started to knit in a tangled web, thread by thread. It wasn't a flashing realisation, but rather a gradual, steady dawning. I was able. I was here to stay.

However, Bangalore assured that the equilibrium wasn't challenging to keep. My PG apartment had its difficulties: the constant heat, the nightly disappearance of my most-loved yoghurt from the fridge, and the landlord's sudden "inspections." My first experience was negotiating with vegetable vendors, riding the Byzantine BMTC bus route, and being a stand-up comedian in line. Every little victory, such as fixing a leaky tap using YouTube assistance to complete my own tax returns, was a moment of silence in becoming an adult. I was no longer an employee or a student. I was a resident of the city, taking part in the city's daily, raunchy ballet.

One evening, sitting at our most-loved terrace area with a cup of tea at the office, gazing at the million illuminations of the town stretching into the dark, Arjun said, "Looks like a circuit board, doesn't it? We all have little lights that blink in and out, trying to establish connections." He was using it as a joke about technology; however, it struck me in the heart. We were doing. Connecting to work with each other and to ourselves. Bangalore is the board that was circuit-board while we were the live stream, sometimes sputtering, occasionally shining bright, yet forever a part of the vital, turbulent flow.

THE MONSOON WITHIN – DOUBTS AND THE WHISPER OF MORE

What I learned was that success isn't a goal, but an environment. In the midst of my hard-earned stability, a new unease was beginning to sprout. It started slowly, in the periods of calm. My now-comfortable commute, staring at the endless construction, new steel skeletons constantly looking up, I'd ask myself: Is growth only vertical? Is it possible to make it broad, horizontal, and different from the routines I'd worked to create so long to appear sometimes like soft cages? It was as if the "idiot friends" became family, and families, too, can cause you to contemplate the world outside of the confines of your home.

The trigger was a telephone call to my parents. The conversation was a whirlwind of my work assignments to the forthcoming Ganesh Chaturthi celebrations in our town. My father, a man with only a few words, stated, "You've conquered the chaos and chaos, beta. The city is in your blood right now. Remember, the heart of India beats in multiple chambers. My Mother and I have both been reading about the latest industries within Maharashtra... Just an idea."

Maharashtra. The word was not an idea, but an echo. It reopened early memories of reading about the caves at Ajanta, the majesty of the Gateway of India, and the literary festivals in Pune. A new kind of energy, historically significant, layered, vast, and pulsing, emanated from that name. My comfortable rhythm of Bangalore life suddenly changed to a syncopated beat.

I started to hear my inner voice whispering, "more." When I was in bookshops, I would be swept over travelogues of the Western Ghats. I'd see news clippings about the theatre scene in Mumbai or Pune's startup incubators, and be drawn to them. It was confusing and almost ungrateful. Bangalore provided everything

I'd ever wanted: A career, freedom, and an identity, a tribe. Was it not enough?

I spoke to Priya in the evening, in the rain, with the downpour pounding against the cafe's windows, making the outside a blur of watercolours. "I am afraid I'm a liar to the woman I love," I said, my voice barely whispering. "Bangalore. As if I'm planning to part with my lover who has been nothing but kind to me."

Priya, always pragmatic, stirred her cup of coffee. "Bangalore isn't a love," she said softly. "She's the most effective teacher you'll ever meet. The greatest teacher's goal isn't to have students in the classroom for a lifetime. It's to help you use the lessons in other ways." Her words did not remove this guilt. But they transformed the issue into a kind of respect.

The anxiety grew in tandem with my professional expertise. In my job, I was now being entrusted with larger projects, yet the excitement lasted only briefly. That initial "wow" of the corporate world was now a normalisation. I was productive, but was I incensed? This question hung over me like an enigmatic shadow. I began looking at potential opportunities without the desire of my first job hunt, but with the curiosity of a traveller examining a new map. There were a variety of Maharashtra-based jobs spanning different industries, scales, and diverse cultural structures.

On a weekend, I went on an uninitiated trip to Mysore. As I sat in the serene stillness at The Mysore Palace, I had an instant, clear vision. It was not a palace but rather the Chhatrapati Shivaji Terminus in Mumbai. It was a new type of architectural wonder, rich in distinct history. The scene was so vivid it sucked the breath out of me. It was a signal. The student I was, whom Bangalore fostered, was ready for a fresh syllabus.

The most intense moment of clarity, however, was from my own PG patio. The monsoon breeze was cool, smelling of wet earth and the faint scent of the night-blooming flower. Below, the city was a dazzling array made of artificial starry night skies. I relived my experience of that frightened woman on the train platform and the phone that was lost, as well as the first check out, and the laughter of my friends, the solitary victory over the solitude. Bangalore did not just give me a job; it gave me an edge and a voice. It also gave me the ability to hear the purest, most honest whispers from my heart.

I was looking up at the dazzling blue sky and whispered to my city, "I believe I'm prepared." These words floated in the misty air, not to say goodbye, but rather as an affirmation of my growth. The emotion was a tapestry of gratitude so strong it was painful, excitement for the unknown, and the sour, sharp sadness of the impending departure. Bangalore was my home. The time was right to see what it had to offer. It had helped me grow.

THE HORIZON BECKONS – CARRYING BANGALORE WITHIN

The decision, once it is made, is a matter of momentum. The process of saying that I had "idiot acquaintances" was the most challenging part. We enjoyed a last, famous dinner at our favourite restaurant, one where we knew the order that we usually make. We shed tears over butter chicken, laughed until it bordered on hilarious, and made promises over old Rumali rotis. "You're changing your Metro system to Namma into Local," Arjun declared, trying to be a bit smug. Rohan gave me a small collection of poetry. "For the new adventures," he said. Priya simply held my hands. "Go become an ethereal star in the fresh sky," Priya mumbled. The family I had chosen to be with, and leaving them felt like letting a piece of my body be left behind. They also understood their role, as Bangalore has taught us all that stagnation is the actual failure.

The transition from professional to personal was a blur. The decision to leave Axis Bank was bittersweet. My manager, who was the same one who once quizzed me on my mistakes, smiled happily. "We employ for ambitiousness," she said. "It is not ethical to enclose it. Get going and conquer the next mountain." Her blessing was the final, authenticating stamp on my journey.

The process of packing my life in Bangalore into two luggage bags with a couple of boxes was an excavation through my personal transformation. I found the printed and rejected resumes I had from my first month, the scratched bill from a street vendor who offered me chai that horrible day I lost my cellphone, the ticket slip for Ranga Shankara, and a group picture from a party off-site. Every object was a relic of emotions. The city had served as an unrelenting editor, removing my ignorance, my fears, and my reliance on others, leaving behind a story that was stronger, clearer, and more real to *myself.*

The night before, I retraced my route from the station to the first train stop. The same streets felt like the well-worn pages from the book that I had read. I recognised the corner the jasmine seller was in, the spot where the finest gumti to drink tea was located, and the route to the alley that was always scented with incense. The chaos had stopped being overpowering; it was more familiar, almost a musical. I had mastered its rhythms and, as a result, I discovered my own.

The train to Maharashtra left from the exact station where it arrived a little over one year ago. I put my forehead to the cold glass. The Bangalore skyline dipped, and a sparkling diadem was placed lightly over the edge of the horizon. There weren't tears anymore, but a deep, peaceful, tranquil fullness.

"A city doesn't need to verify your proof of identity. It wants your confidence. In return, it tells you an account."

Bangalore was asking for my bravery, and I'd paid it in instalments for each unsuccessful application and lonely evening, every courageous "yes" to an exciting new adventure. In exchange, it had provided me the most amazing tale: my own. It showed me that dreams aren't permanent destinations but living, life-giving things that change over time. Professional fulfilment is useless without personal development, and independence can only be discovered in the relationships that expose you to vulnerability.

I will not leave Bangalore to go back. I carry it in the strength it created and the bonds it forged, in the trust it built out of doubt. It is clear that the "Bangalore Days" aren't over; they form the basis. The chaos is not visible from the outside, but it is an organised and powerful force within me, a motor that keeps me evolving. While the scenery outside the train window changes, my heart beats an unstoppable drum. The next chapter remains unwritten, but the hand holding the pen is stable, steady, and forever engraved by an ethos of the city that is a garden. The story continues.

Maharashtra Journey

LEAVING BEHIND BANGALORE'S DREAMSCAPE

The dawn on June 10th, 2018, was not a simple arrival; it fell over Bangalore like liquid amber, shining on the roofs of my previous. I sat at the foot of the stage, a sculpture of tranquil insanity with seven souls out of cloth and leather luggage. Each contained a small piece of my life, which I was gently, painstakingly taking away. They weren't packed with items, but they were heavy with the weight of time. Bangalore was more than the city I left. It was a love I had to part with, as was my soul, a tally of sorrow and gratitude.

For a long time, this city was my closest friend. The city's crowded, breath-taking streets were the pages on which I wrote my teenage years. The smell of filter coffee from hundreds of little cafes was my daily incense and a holy start to the day, fuelled by impossible dreaming. The monsoon rains wouldn't simply drop; they would hug the earth's sun-baked surface, unleashing the scent of the petrichor, which is the hallmark of Bangalore's passion, a smell that would always whisper to my soul, "Create. Become."

It was a place with stunning duality. It embraced me in the solitary green embrace of Cubbon Park for a while and then slammed me into the pulsing, electric beat that is the Silicon Valley heart the next. I was able to grow between the enduring sounds of a veena in the Chowdiah and the fast-paced clicking of keyboards within glass towers, and between the familiar, fiery pleasure of a roadside masala dosa and the enticing attraction of a delicious plate. Bangalore was the most romantic of my relationships, which was based on lively debates with my acquaintances in traffic-clogged cabs, as well as solitary walks beneath umbrellas of old rain trees, in the quiet satisfaction of having a problem resolved, or a promotion that was earned, and a part of me was discovered.

The train's whistle. A loud, silvery sound that cut through my thoughts. It was not a rebuke; it was a call. The moment I got on the train, the metallic groaning sound of the coach was the bend of an old-fashioned timeline. I settled down near the window and put my hand against the glass with an unintentional, final, and futile kiss.

> ***"We are a mosaic of the areas that love us,"* I whispered to myself, the personal truth I created in this departure. *"We don't perish; we simply change the tile so that we can see an entirely different view."***

As the city began to slide away first in chunks, then in flashes, then in a blurred streak of green and grey, the rhythmic chant of the wheels on the tracks became a mantra: *you-carry-it-with-you, you-carry-it-with-you.* The urban sprawl softened into the countryside, a visual echo of my own emotional transition. I was suspended in between chapters, the ink on the previous one still wet, and the next one is a terrifying, thrilling blank.

My thoughts were racing towards Pune. What stories were buried within the walls of its past? What changes would take over the streets of its city and my own life? I was thinking of Srinivas Mishra, who was soon to be the face of the world and a voice. Presence. He was a promise to welcome in the midst of uncertainty and a possible anchor in the coming tidal wave of change. The anticipation was an emotional flutter and a mix of fear and undiluted, bright faith.

The trip itself was the release. With each mile that passed, I felt the gentle loss of sagging skin. The young lady who had been a visitor to Bangalore some time ago, with big eyes and shaky hopes, was transformed by the city into a woman with grit and a calmer confidence. The woman now crossed an edging, not letting go of her history, yet allowing her future to join her halfway.

Dawn broke again as we walked towards Pune, and the sky was smoky with delicate oranges and pinks of the new day. The light didn't seem like a closing but rather an opening. Train, the instrument of transformation, slowed down its music.

I put my bags in a pile, and each bag was lighter in spirit. When I got on the new platform, the air was scented of stone that had been sun-baked and potential that was still undefined. I took a deep, steadying breath.

Bangalore, my dearest dreamscape, slipped away into a gilded memory by the galleries of my heart. Pune stood before me as a story waiting for the first word. And I, the writer of my personal love memoir that includes people and places, took the pen in hand, with my heart open, waiting to get in love again.

A MEETING WITH FATE

My story does not start with a grand statement and a sluggish rhythm, the metallic sigh that sounds like train wheels against the track as they decelerate, marking the conclusion of a movement and the uncertain, hopeful beginning of a new one. I stood in front of the door, and the sweltering Pune air, full of the prospect of monsoons and the possibility, was rushing towards me. In front of me, the ghostly silhouette of Bangalore, the city of soft memories and cherished dreams, slipped into the past. I snatched one, uneasy thought in my chest: "We are never merely leaving. We are always waiting hungry, on the doorstep of our future self."

It was more than just a location, but was a living thing. It breathed and roared; it performed a raucous symphony of arrival. Porters yelled in brisk Marathi, and while the wheels of a suitcase clicked, the smoky, melodious sound of boiling tea and the aroma of crispy snacks wafted throughout. In the midst of a sea of unidentified faces, I was in a state of complete isolation. I was just a single word lost in a fast-paced novel. Then I was able to see him.

Srinivas. He wasn't huge; however, he carried a smug confidence that outlined a calm oasis amid the chaos. His smile wasn't an erupting smile; it was a gradual, rising recognition, as if the man was waiting not only to see me but that *model* of me who could step off that train. "Welcome to Pune," he said in a warm baritone, which escaped my ears and settled into my nerves. His handshake was solid, a tangible anchor. With a single touch, the terrifying idea of "a new beginning" began to take shape, becoming something concrete and tangible, guided.

He shuffled my seven suitcases, each one an obelisk for a previous self, with effortless grace. As I followed him through the crowd, I did not feel like an observer, but rather an earth searching for its sun, sucked into a peaceful orbit. The city exploded out of the windows of his car; it was an edgy, chaotic tapestry. It was 7 am, which meant that Pune was already in full, beautiful throat. The smoky smell that sparked from the spiced *vada pav* and the sweet aroma of *jalebis* were ablaze and mixed. Light reflected off rainbow-colored saris hanging from shopfronts, transforming streets into vibrant rivers. Auto-rickshaws, adorned with the colours of bright beetles, sped through the city, and their horns spoke their own language.

This sensory immersion was awe-inspiring. However, Srinivas's solitary presence beside me was an effective filter. He transformed this chaos into poetry. "Listen," he seemed to say in a solitary voice, "this isn't noise. It's the city's heartbeat. It's now yours to enjoy too."

My new residence is in Viman Nagar. In the first evening when the sun set orange and rose over the skyline, I sat on my tiny balcony. A gentle breeze of jasmine whispered the secrets of the past hidden within these walls. Below, the neighbourhood pulsated with a mellow duality: contemporary cafes humming amid old-fashioned banyan trees; joggers wearing athletic clothes strolled past older women wearing saris with nine yards. It was an area where history did not stand in opposition to contemporarily, but danced alongside it. My heart, full of excitement and fear, was now part of the dance.

Srinivas has been my own personal bridge. He wasn't an expert on excursions; he was more of a curator of experiences that revealed the city's innermost thoughts and my own. The bike ride we took together is etched in my mind as an esoteric text. When I was seated behind him, the world was an ebb and flow of sensation. A breeze was like a charming partner, taking my breath away while we drove through the streets. We stood before the majestic, silent, bleak ruins of Shaniwar Wada, its walls telling of grandeur and tales of ghosts. In stark contrast, we glided through the lush, Bohemian lanes of Koregaon Park, and the air was filled with coffee and the spirit of creativity.

At the renowned Vohuman Cafe, he ushered me into the sacred rite of Bun Masha and Iranian Chai. The sweet, strong tea was much more than an alcoholic beverage; it was a sacrament that signified belonging. The butter began to melt on the bread, and my resistance grew, so did mine. I turned to him, his eyes wide with smiles as he spoke about the local legends, and I observed a shift in a tectonic plate of emotion, accelerating in a way that could not be reversed. This was more than just a guideline. It was a shared experience between the worlds.

The rains poured in just as they have always in Pune and transformed Pune into a shimmering watercolour-like dream. In the evening, engulfed in the midst of a torrential downpour, we raced through the slippery streets of FC Road, taking refuge under a bright cover of umbrellas at the *Chaat* vendor. The spicy taste in *the pani puri* was a constant in the air, with the fiery tamarind water was a roar of excitement upon the tongue. On my side, Srinivas's dress was pinned to his shoulders, his hair was dripping with laughter, his laughter ringing over the rumbling rain. In that ordinary, magical moment in the midst of the smoot of food and the symphony from the storm, I became awestruck, not in an extravagant gesture, but rather with the comfort of sharing laughter amid the sprinkles of rain. I was in love with the guy who taught me that wandering is the best way to locate a spot as well as yourself.

In this new perspective, it was not an obstacle to my self-discovery journey; it was actually the primary driving force. With Srinivas, I was able to explore more. He facilitated my development and stumble, but also to blossom. I learned bits of Marathi, not from a textbook, but through bargaining with vegetable vendors, with their amused eyes. I was awestruck by one of my own Ganesh Chaturthi celebrations, soaking up the deafening, joyful swell of parades and feeling the collective fervour ringing in my chest. In the quiet evenings, we would stroll along the river Mula-Mutha and watch its swift waters reflect the city's lights, as we talked of everything and nothing about our memories, our naive fantasies, the peaceful hope we could not even call.

My tiny PG space became a refuge where I shed my former skin. Within the walls of that room, I was able to master the math of being independent. I discovered that being alone could be therapeutic, that being in my personal company was not a punishment but rather a privilege. When loneliness threatened, Srinivas was there not to help me solve it, but to join me as I struggled. His presence was a peaceful testimony to the fact that I was loved and loved, just the way I am.

Pune was no longer just a backdrop. It became a part of our story, the scene of our advancement. The smell of dusty books that were smuggled into second-hand bookstores, the peaceful green horizon in the Osho Gardens, and the intellectual energy of the colleges, all these elements became rooms within the home of our life together. In the city of Bangalore, its gorgeous and swollen heart, its ferocious energy and sudden pockets of tranquillity, mirrors my personal change. I was no longer the woman who had quit Bangalore and was trembling with anxious desire. I was being written over in a word-by-word fashion day by day through love, by challenges, and the overwhelming determination of this city.

When I reflect on it from a position of peace and contentment, I realize that my life's fate isn't a lightning strike. It's a delicate, inevitable mixture of trim options: the possibility to take a flight and accept a help offer, to sample a new food, to smile when it rains, or to trust in a stranger who feels like home. Srinivas was my destiny, not because he was meant for me, but because with him, I gained the confidence to fulfil my destiny.

This is our story as a trifecta: The city, the man, and the girl I was between them. Pune is the earth, Srinivas was the steady sunlight that nourished him, while I became the one who was finally brave enough to break in search of the sunlight. It's a love story about two hearts who recognise each other at a bustling station. It is also a history of a soul's journey to the Renaissance.

This is why I write this in a tribute to that convergence, the magical alchemy that takes place when you're brave enough to leap into the unknown only to discover that it's been waiting for a long time with a smile, and with a hand stretched out, ready to take you not only to a new home, but also to the home inside you that you didn't know you could have.

"The greatest journey," **as I penned in my journal the first night of rain,** ***"is not measured in miles from here up to this point, but instead in the infinite distance you travel in one soul, which can make it feel as if the world is the home, it is."***

AN INVITATION TO BELONG

It is said that a city can keep the memories of an entire heartbeat. For me, the city that holds that memory is Pune. My story, and our story, is not recorded in the smallest of minutes, but rather in the scent of its rains, the pulsing chaotic streets of the city, and the serene stillness of its mornings. This isn't just the recollection of a moment; it's the story of a heart discovering its true home, witness to the moment when an invitation to be part of the community was whispered to me, and I, in all my being, accepted it.

My relationship with Pune and his family began on his birthday. Not any birthday, but mine on June 15, 2018. I was expecting cake and maybe a few of my friends. What I got was an experience that was a welcome. Srinivas, along with his entire family, orchestrated a surprise concert that turned into a party that felt more like a celebration and a welcome home. The air was suffused with the scent of incense and promises. Rangoli patterns lit up like smiles on thresholds of stone, and their hues a ferocious happiness over the ground. The music wasn't only heard, it was felt through the soles of our feet, a pulsating rhythm that seemed to come from the city's ancient centre.

The next day, I realised that celebration is an expression of language. It's the language of resilience, the language of shared histories. At the heart of all this was Srinivas, his solitary eyes looking at me with wonder and giving me a slice of his life without saying a word. The meal was a narrative on plates. Every flavour, the tang of sol kadhi, the warmth of bharli vangi and the sweet, fragrant saffron-kissed closing of shrikhand, was a phrase in a narrative about home, harvest and the past. I tasted more than food; I tasted lineage. When the soft shrikhand began to melt onto my tongue, I came across a thought that is now the foundation for my heart: ***"The most profound love stories are not just written in letters, but seasoned in family recipes and served with the silent understanding that to share a meal is to share a life."*** At that time, my body didn't grow a year older; I was being woven through, thread by thread, into a richer, more vibrant tapestry.

The warm glow of the birthday celebration was the solitary, unstoppable dawn of our lives. Pune was our canvas. The everyday and the grand depicted our relationship. We were avid explorers of corners and crevices, avid drinkers of chai on the streets that tasted like monsoon and were mysterious. I recall the pounding of the people on FC Road, the stolen laugh that avada Pav the sweet, sticky taste of a jalebi we ate with our hands, rubbing in a quieter way than the city's roar, but still awe-inspiring to my senses.

We sought out the past, too, by exploring the solemn archways in the Aga Khan Palace and the mysterious ruin of Shaniwar Wada. In the midst of those stones, I was able to feel the heat of the past; however, beside him, I was able to feel the euphoria in the numbness of a future being constructed. He would show me a sculpture and speak in low reverence, and I was in love, not just with the historical record but also with the man who was awed by the past. Then, Sinhagad was there. Our place of refuge. It was a joy to climb its steps in early morning darkness, with a breathless optimism for the reward of an unmistakably beautiful sunrise that glowed over the earth below. In the vast, solitary space, as the sun sat on our companions' faces, we shared our dreams that seemed as limitless as the landscape. He was my peace and steady companion to my whirling emotions. On a night, sitting on his terrace, city lights glistening like a spangled galaxy below, he walked over to me. The sound of Pune gave way to a dull hum. He looked me in the eyes and not just at me, but told me, "Let us begin something wonderful." Five words. An anchor. A genesis.

Our anticipation for our wedding was tangible, hanging in the air like a sweet. Every glance we exchanged became promises; every conversation sounded like the weight of unspoken words from July 15 July 15, 2018. I felt as if I was walking on a gorgeous cliff, with one foot in the beloved past we'd crafted and the other positioned to enter a promising future.

The action moved to Bhubaneswar, my hometown of temples, to perform the conclusion of our prelude. The city was dressed to impress. It seemed lively and enthusiastic. July 15 began not in silence, however, but with a calm sound in my soul. As I stood before the mirror, I was in a lehenga with embroidered dreams. The silk sang with every move and reflected the light as if it were the tiniest of laughter. The hair flowers were more than just decorations. They were a fragrant affirmation. I was a familiar reflection, but an entirely new woman on the verge of her best-ever transformation. Then I looked at her and told her, "This is finally happening."

The location was a vision that was realised. The hall was transformed into a lush garden with soft lighting and cascading flowers, and the air was scented with jasmine and excitement. A gentle strum from the love song, woven into the conversation of loved voices of family and friends and the chorus of our duet. My heart beat like a drum against my ribs.

Then I was able to see him. Srinivas, seated in a serene position amid the soft light, clad in a traditional sexiness, His calm lay in a quiet, deep pool. However, his eyes... his eyes were filled with affection, focused solely on me. Moving toward him felt like the easiest and most meaningful trip that I have ever taken. The world was blurred at the edges. The only clear thing was the way to him. Each step was a silent pledge and a surrender of my personal self to what would become the "us."

We sat together, our hands shaking, when we saw one another. His touch brought me home. The rituals began with a stunning ancient ritual of blessings and symbols, which rooted our love for each other in the ancient soil. Then, the moment. The world was awestruck. He took the ring as an easy, perfect circular promise.

"With this ring," he declared, his voice strong and full of emotion that echoed in the sacred space that we share, "I offer my heart. I promise you my yesterday, my tomorrow and every future that my soul can ever experience. I have chosen you, in the midst of everything we cherish, I choose you to be my partner, my love and my forever."

The tears, the honest betrayers of joy, poured across my face. My voice echoed in a soft, unwavering tone. "With this ring," I whispered, my eyes at his, "I promise my love and devotion to you forever. I promise you my faith and my hopes, as well as the promise to be with you and grow with you and find an abode in your eyes throughout the course that I live."

As he put the ring on my finger as a physical representation of an unbreakable connection, a roar of pure joy swept across me. It was a sensation so overwhelming that my body could not contain the euphoria of joy, relief, and a deep, soul-felt feeling of rightness. The roar of applause was more than just a sound, it was an act of blessing and an euphoric celebration of the union now sealed through the love of witnesses and love.

In that glistening moment, in the midst of the faces of our standard time, I was able to comprehend everything. The day of my birthday in Pune, as well as the monsoons and the fort in the morning, and the peaceful evenings were all chapters that led to this perfect sentence. Our wedding was much more than a formality. It was a living thing, born of the shared chai and whispered fantasies and now blessed by tradition and cherished by the love of our lives.

Pune has given me a sense of community. Bhubaneswar gave me a stage. However, Srinivas, my peace and wonder, my partner, told me the story. As we embraced the future, it unfolded before us, not as a road that was not yet known; instead, it was a path of sunshine that we were already beginning to walk along, together, our hearts pounding in a beat that was, and will forever be, exclusively and forever ours. The invitation was accepted. The relationship was now permanent.

LOVE'S JOURNEY THROUGH LIFE'S TRIALS

Love is said to build cathedrals of its own, not from spires and stones instead, but from the smallest of small moments of silence. My church was just a humble flat located on the wrong side of Pune's fast-paced heartbeat. For most, this was just a home amid concrete, but for me, it was the sacred ground where my journey with Srinivas began. Every Friday night when the city sucked in its daily sigh, I would embark on my journey. The jumble of roaring scooters, screaming vendors, and radios blaring was not a source of inconvenience on these drives but rather a barrier I had to cross to reach my dream destination. Every mile, the sound would diminish in my head, only to be replaced by a booming anthem of excitement. When I arrived at the street, my heart would make the same familiar dance. I'd park, gaze at the window that was already sparkling with the gentle, buttery glow of the lamp he'd switched off for me. I would then think: *Here, time doesn't go by, and it never ends.*

It was like entering the warm, quiet exhale. The rumble of the city vanished to be replaced by a peaceful sound that was only for us. His home was distinguished by the magnificent windows, which framed the Pune sky as a living painting. The most memorable moments of our lives were painted in the deep purples and golds of the sunset. Srinivas stood in silhouette against the dying light, and I felt an euphoria so powerful it took my breath away. This was not just romance; it was a deep cell-based recognition. With him, I wasn't only loved but *acknowledged*. We'd talk for hours in a reclining position on the couch, and our conversations ranged from the serious to the ridiculous. Our space wasn't bare. It was charged with a gentle euphoria of understanding. I wrote in a notebook I kept within my wallet: ***"Love is not two people looking at each other, but two people looking out from the same sanctuary, watching the world turn together."*** This was us. We were co-conspirators in a shady, peaceful, tranquil world.

The rituals we performed were holy. We cooked together, and it became our sacred, unspoken ritual. The kitchen, which was small and often overheated, became our holy space. I can still feel the sizzle of cumin seeds sizzling in hot oil, taste the sourness of ginger and garlic, and feel the steam from the boiling rice in our eyes. "Today, it's my turn!" I'd shout, holding a ladle in the shape of a sceptre, and launching into the new recipe with theatrical energy. He'd be my sous chef, cutting onions with an accuracy that made me laugh. Our elbows are moving, our laughter spicing this dish better than any other spice. We would share the tastes of an old wooden spoon with our gazes merging with the steam. Later, sitting down to eat that meal at the window, with the city lights glistening in the distance like stars, was more than just a meal; it was the moment of communion. Every taste was a memory that was in the making.

However, even the most sacred places of worship are not invincible to the whims of the soul. The first shadow fell so softly I thought it was an unintentional cloud. An ice-cold glass sat in his hands more often in our golden hour. It was initially an accompaniment to his slumber, an amber gemstone that caught the sun's light. I didn't think much of it as an individual unwinding after an extended week. What a fool that is now.

The transformation was gradual; it was a gradual, quiet change in our world. One glass was replaced by two. The weekend ritual started earlier on Saturday and began to take over Friday night. A bottle called Old Monk, once a regular fixture on the shelves, was beginning to move at a brand-new rapidity. I recall one night with a particular, painful clarity. I was sitting at the stove stirring up an oozing dish of *pav Bhaji* with my husband, and the air was filled with the smell of butter and mashed vegetables. In the kitchen, it was cozy and full of the soothing sound of our shared love. I turned to make a joke about the potatoes, then saw him standing at the counter, facing me, drinking the drink. The issue wasn't with the act itself; it was the slight hunch of his shoulders and the quick turn of the bottle, which sent a cold drip down my spine. The sun that day was bloody orange. It flowed down the windows as it set the liquid inside the glass ablaze.

"Is everything alright, my love?" I asked my voice to be less tinny than I had intended and almost lost it in the smoky sizzle from the pan.

He turned, and the smile he offered me was one that I loved, but it didn't reach his eyes. They wore an ethereal, glassy sheen, reminiscent of windows that opened onto a room where I wasn't welcome anymore. "Of course," he stated, his words were smooth and practised. "It's the way I unwind. Don't be worried about your beautiful head."

Don't fret. Those two words were the basis of my disintegration. Every worry I expressed was gently dismissed, twisted into a story of work stress or the need for me to "just take the edge off." My lover, who was his home, became an audience in a performance I couldn't comprehend. We were in a state of silence. Became more ferocious, not filled with peace and comfort, but rather with the silence of. I was devastated and not just by one moment, but by the slow, painful realisation that the person I loved was on an uninvolved journey through an unknown place that I couldn't follow. The trust and transparency that had been the basis of our relationship became like shifting sand. My mind was lost in the forest of my own anxieties, without a compass.

The emotional tapestry that was created in those days was a painful triptych of terror, anxiety and a pain that was so severe it was physical.

Confusion was an endless maze. At one point, I saw my Srinivas toying with me, pulling me into a dance across the floor of our living room to music we could only hear. A stranger was watching his eyes. I would lie in bed at night, reliving our conversations and scouring for clues I had missed. Did it have to do with me? Was it an accident? Did there exist a sadness in his past that he never discussed? My mind was locked in endless loops of questions with no answers.

Then, be afraid of the cold, slithering friend. This wasn't just a fear of arguments or discontent. It was a primal, terrifying fear of eroding. Every drink was like a swell that swept over the base of our common cathedral and slowly removed particles of sand from *his*. I was worried about the glow in his eyes and his health, given the direction we painted with such vivid colours during our sunset talks. The most important thing was that I was terrified of the silence. The lively conversations that would go on for hours would occasionally morph into a silence in which he seemed to be a galaxy away, and the smack of his glass being the only sound.

The pain in my heart was a continuous, dull ache that sat beneath my breastbone. It was the ache of watching a loved book gradually fade in the sunlight. It was a feeling of love so passionate, yet I was unable to touch the person. The love we shared was bittersweet, always tinged by the lingering taste of what might be hiding beneath the surface. I cried for our peaceful past while I held on to our tense present.

In the most savage sadness, a germinating seed of hope would not go away. It was fragile, which was fed by memories. I clung to the man who rescued the last mango for me. He understood what I had taken my tea without question, his permission, and whose laughter could be heard on those rare, sober early mornings, filling the room with the pure, infectious sound. I was convinced, with a belief that defied all logic, that the bond we had created was more than the shadow. When words did not work like they often did, I relied on the faith that was my sole source of support.

In the midst of personal chaos, the more critical issue of our future began as a whisper and then a shout. Marriage. In our society, it's never an issue of mere curiosity. It's a convergence of two river families' history, expectations, and histories. My heart was aching to be a part of that union, the official, holy sanction of what I felt within my heart. I imagined our lives not in a brand-new, large, luxurious house in the middle of nowhere, but in our sanctuary, forming an intimate family amid sunsets and the recognizable cracks in the ceiling.

However, how do I see a future when my moment was so uncertain? The shadow of his drink sat on our dining table like an unwelcome guest. Was it possible to swear "for better or for worse" even though it was clear that the "worse" was already here, drinking quietly from a glass tucked away in the corner? My family's expectations were a burden. What would I do to introduce him to? How do I explain the occasional look of disinterest or the slight shift in mood? It's a private act of rebellion; however, marriage is an open declaration. Was our love sufficient to stand up to not just the pressures of life and tribulations, but also the public scrutiny?

It was the time when the Nag Panchami festival began, with a day of vibrant, serpentine energy sweeping through the city. Additionally, it was Srinivas's birthday. The air felt different, filled with devotion, incense and a frantic celebration of rebirth and security. I began to prepare and set out to create the perfect day that would be a source of calm and happiness. I decorated my apartment with marigolds, their acrid, optimistic scent competing with the hazy, faint whiskey scent that sometimes pervaded the air.

The evening was a time when our closest friends crowded into the apartment, joyous and well-wishing. The space was cozy, with friends' camaraderie, and festive desserts were passed around as stories revolved. Srinivas was at the centre of the room, and the host was charming, smiling widely. However, my love was an observer of his subtleties. I noticed the tiny tremors in his hands as he made a toast to his guests, not champagne-based but the darker, stronger beverage. I could see the way his laughter went on for an entire beat as his eyes would wander around the room before landing with a sense of relief at the bottle on the sideboard. I saw the fleeting, anxious glance exchanged by two of our most cherished acquaintances, a quiet confirmation that my fears weren't phantoms of an overactive imagination.

In the moment, amid crowds and celebrations, I felt a deep sense of loneliness. The love of my life celebrated his birthday, and I was grieving for the death of someone sitting right in front of me. The gold hues of our church were dim, the space felt vulnerable, almost as though laughter and clinking glasses could break it. I was looking at Srinivas, his face lit by candlelight, and my heart broke in two. One part of me loved him with a passion that scared me. The other half was perched on the edge, pondering whether our story of love was a recollection of the building of the perfect paradise or a eulogy for the loss of a loved one, sip by sip, drink by drink, at the exact location we called home. The journey wasn't finished, but the deeper dusk obscured the road ahead.

BEFORE THE VOWS

My story is not just about an event; it is a journey. It's a story told not in ink but through the footsteps of a stone, in prayers sung in silence, and in the peaceful, powerful, earth-shattering force of a bond that holds your feet even when the world tries to sway you. This is the story of my heart during the time it realized that the most enduring bonds aren't sealed with gold, but are forged in resilience.

Our trip to Bhimasankar was conceived in an era of quiet. Srinivas, whose eyes have always been awestruck by the serenity of a deep lake, suggested it wasn't an excursion but rather an analogy. "Let's begin our life not from a threshold, but from a trail," he said, his hands wrapped around mine. "Let's earn our blessings step by step." And that's how we set out two souls, trading the plain, flat and predictable lands of our lives for the arduous and chilly ascent to the heavens.

It was like a concertina of our contrasting characteristics. While I was rushing, he was at a deliberate speed. While I was focused on the top of the mountain, he spotted an unidentified wildflower stuck against a chip in the stone. "Look," he'd murmur, "persistence in the most fragile form." Every effortful breath, every slip of loose gravel, and each shared drink of water from the same bottle felt like an emulation of what marriage could be: intense, lasting and deeply intimate the physical tension dissolved into a bizarre, exhilarating union. Our distinct pasts, my work-related worries, and his solitary, methodical approach disappeared with every step upward, like weights tossed aside. We were becoming one entity, a "we" with a shared rhythm and a shared goal.

"A pilgrimage is the heart's way of mapping eternity onto mortal ground."

I wrote the note in my journal that evening before we left without knowing just how true it would be. Bhimasankar wasn't just an area; it was an ever-living altar to the passage of the eternal time. As we finally entered the temple and emerged from a haze of silver and cool mist, the entire world quieted. The ancient edifice, small and mighty in the unending green of the Sahyadris, humbled me to the deepest core. It has witnessed centuries of dawns, of love, of human hopes, and would now be witness to us.

The air was dense and filled not only of incense, but of the possibility of. The smell of crushed marigolds and jasmine from the offerings was in our lungs and a sweet promise. With our hands in the air, we lay down on the sandstone that had been worn. I closed my eyes, and the noise of my mind about wedding lists and the upcoming doubts ceased. In that deep silence, the prayer I offered wasn't a plea but more of a seed. Let our love last as long as the mountains. Let our love be as strong as these old stones. Let our joys rise as this mist, and let our strength be like the bedrock that lies beneath us. I noticed Srinivas's thumb tracing a circle on my palm, and he said a silent amen. At that point, the time didn't slow down; it rolled over us and woven our quiet vows into the structure of the space. We weren't just a couple who fell in love; we were an agreement, made by silence and stone.

This descent was awash with a golden, dreamlike tranquillity. Srinivas was smiling, his face softened by the afternoon light, and he was looking at me when he said, with an unsettling sound I felt in my heart, "This is only the start, you know." It was a promise that resonated throughout my heart's valleys. We felt joyful and euphoric, carrying the temple's grace in our hearts and ready to walk into our sunny future.

Then, the crack.

The fall didn't come from a mountain path; it was from a cliff of safety. After returning to the holy Ash of Bhimasankar for a few days, I received the phone call. The department that was my workplace, the brainchild that was nurtured from a flimsy concept into a living, breathing, breath-taking entity, was going to be defunct. The company's language was uninspiring, business-like "restructuring," "synergy," "strategic withdrawal." For me, they sounded like only one, resounding word: obsolete.

The shock was a physical one. I was in my office, the same one where Rashmi and I had planned a series of revolutions over endless cups of tea and shivered as the foundations of my self-identity crumbled. Rashmi. A mentor and ally who was my most formidable professional adversary. Our perspectives were diverging violently, with her relentless expansion versus my cautious consolidation. The once-easy collaboration was now sunk into an unsettling trench war between spreadsheets and simmering animosity. However, when the day of reckoning was reached, there was no explosion, just a horrible, empty silence. We stared at each other through the space, and I did not see an evictee, a villain, or a casualty. The bitterness that I had hoped to taste was not there, but was being replaced by the ash of shared sorrow. We had constructed a vessel together, and we were now able to witness it sinking by the very same lifeboat.

However, the professional shipwreck wasn't the only beginning. The tsunami slammed into my personal shores with brutal force. The wedding was just a few weeks away. It was a matter of time. Shaadi cards, elegantly embossed and stunning, were tucked away in a box like a mocking artifact from the past, which was no longer mine. What could I do to walk down across the jaimala aisle, glowing and safe, while my body felt like a shell that a bank had smashed? The pride that has always been my silent companion was shrivelling. I had always envisioned getting married to Srinivas as a partner who would not only bring happiness but also stability. Now, I felt like a liability a question mark. In the dark, silent hours of the night, the voice of a cruel man whispered, "What do you have today? A drained bank account and broken compass?

The script that society's unconscious plays on a loop in my head. The worth of a woman, subtle yet firmly, is frequently tied to her ability to perform. I was no longer a successful professional; I was a likely bride-to-be who had been fired. The embarrassment was a hot cloak that I couldn't get rid of. I resisted calls, fearing the well-meaning, pathetic "How are you, really?" I observed my parents' concerned glances, carefully concealed amid wedding conversations, and each of them felt like a pinprick to my heart.

I turned away. A woman who had hiked mountains struggled to get out of her bed. The rousing prayer of Bhimasankar, "Let us journey last..." seemed like a childish reflection of a long but foolish past. The mist in the air was mysterious, and now, a cloud of desperation sank into my thoughts.

In all of it, there was Srinivas.

He didn't make any changes. He didn't bombard me with empty nonsense or uninteresting job leads. He was just anchored.

A star-lit night, on the balcony of my home, the weight of the world was unbearably heavy. The wedding luxuries inside looked like a costume for a show I was no longer able to perform in. I lay there, wrapped in a cold shiver that no shawl could keep me warm, the cold, silent tears. He found me. He didn't say, "Don't cry." He didn't even mention, "It will be okay." He sat next to me, put his arm around me and slid my head over my shoulder. We sat in the dark, in silence, absorbing the distant noise from the town and a universe that swayed in silence.

After a few minutes, the soft, steady voice broke the silence. "Do you remember the third turn on the Bhimasankar path?" the man asked. "The one with the sheer rock face, where the chain was anchored?"

I smiled at him. I was confused.

"You went first," continued the man. "You tried every link, every foothold before you said to me, 'It's strong. Follow me. You weren't averse to risk. You were cautious. You were a good leader." He stopped with his breath, warming through my locks. "This is our rock face. And I'm following you. This is not the person who holds the job title. The one who is testing the chains. The one whose strength lies in her steadfastness. We're not climbing it for the blessing of a temple. We're climbing it for ourselves. We will make it through this. Together."

His words were a lifeline given to me, not to save me from falling, but to join me in the dark, new darkness. He changed the way I told my story. I wasn't an unemployed executive; I was a skilled climber in a brand-new, rugged landscape. He helped me to see my own strength in his steadfast eyes.

In the days that followed, his love was practical poetry. He rethought our wedding spending plan with me, not as a serious exercise but as an opportunity to work together for our future. "Fewer flowers, more everlasting memories," he'd tell me and make me smile with tears in my eyes. He transformed my job search from a panicked search into a mission shared by all and a belief in me that was an unwavering, gentle breeze at my back.

The wedding was here. When I wore the gold and red, I felt a distinct weight, not from shame but of profound, hard-earned grace. The attire that he wore was not only a symbol of marriage, but it was also an official seal to the vow that we had made.

We've made it to each other by stepping on the rock. After our seven rounds, or pheras, each step was a testimony not to a perfect beginning but to a foundation tested and proved indestructible. The group had already made their trip. It was a celebration.

In retrospect, from a position of peace and a new work, I can see the story of the year. Bhimasankar offered us the symbolism, the holy blueprint for a journey shared by all. The loss of a job was the unexpected storm, the avalanche that swept across our way. And Srinivas's devotion was the indefatigable belief that the way was the one that we chose for each other, step after carefully taken step, was the way to get there.

The love story we tell isn't the fairy tale of unending bliss. It's a tale of pilgrimage. It tells the story of vows not only before the divine witnesses in the mountain fog, but also in the quiet of a balcony shared by two people, when you are in the grip of fear and the firm grip of a hand that cannot be let go. This is an example of how the most romantic gesture isn't the grand gesture in the perfect moment, rather, it is the calm, day choice to see you as a climber with your spouse, as all they can see is the crunch.

"We did not marry in a temple of stone, but in the temple we built together on the path between two heartbeats: one of hope, and one of holding on."

A DAY OF LOVE

The Unfolding Dream

There is a unique attraction to waiting for a wedding day you have painted over and over in the still gallery of your heart. Our wedding was more than an event, it was the culmination of a symphony created through whispers, shared gazes and the quiet, constant beat of two hearts that beat together. For this crescendo, we chose a timeless, elegant backdrop: Swosti Premium Hotel. Swosti Premium Hotel. It's easy to say that we decided it because the wrong one is a boring verb. It was more about how Swosti was presented as an unfinished chapter in an unwritten book we were meant to fill. From the moment we stepped into the grand lobby with crystal chandeliers that hung like frozen tears and cast a warm, honeyed glow over marble floors that showed our happy faces, we were certain. This wasn't only a place to be; it was the beginning of a chapter of our lifetime.

The following weeks were a breathtaking, beautiful blur, a tapestry of threads of careful planning and awe-inspiring emotions. Time, that elusive thing, played tricks. It was dragging its feet throughout the fittings, with each pin-prick being a reminder of the formality that was to follow, but then it raced in a frenzied manner as December approached, with us fumbling for times in an attempt to slow the dawn. My wedding gown was more than just a gown. It was a place of thread and silk. I can remember slipping it on in the last fitting, and the weight of beautiful embroidery, each stitch a prayer in silence, each design a tale told by skilled artisans. It was not just on my shoulders but also on my heart. It was a story of heritage and the future interspersed. I looked into my mirror to see more than just a bride; she was actually stepping into the past of love as I felt the soft fingers of my parents that guided me. Srinivas, with his perfectly designed suit, was my saviour. His elegance was never cold. It was a calm, confident appeal that was like whispering, "I am in the room. I am ready. For you, for us."

"Love can be described as the meticulous plan of a thousand small things to ensure that two souls are in a perfect place just to be together."

The Palace Awakes

December 9th, 2018. The day didn't start until, but it arrived in full force with a stunning work revealed. Swosti changed into something else. Swosti was now more than a grand hotel and grandeur, but a palace alive with a soul of its own. Halls were adorned with rich textiles that sparkled like jewel-like liquid tones. The air itself was scented with the heady, sweet smell of flowers set in intricate designs that appeared to blossom from pure happiness. The light fixtures... Oh, the lights. They did not shine through wires, but rather out of the atmosphere itself, caught by the greenery and reflected on shining surfaces, creating a dreamlike arrangement laid out only for the day. It was a breathtaking scene of romanticism, a landscape crafted with such care and precision that it felt like an extension of our own emotions.

The ceremony was like a heartbeat. A sacred and a suspended breath. Standing in front of Srinivas, the world, the grand hall, the adored faces, the fragrant flowers all disintegrated into a calming centre. It was just him. His eyes, which were encircling mine, were a world I was eager to explore for the rest of my life. In that silence before taking the vows, I could hear the sound of every laugh as well as the memory of each ease, the promise of every future we'd ever discussed. Then, the vows came in. Our vows. They were not words from scripts, but lived things that we breathed into existence. My voice, not shaken out of fear, but in the enormity of the truth, I promised him my present and every day of my life. I pledged to be his home and adventurer, to support his hopes like they were my own, to be his unwavering support throughout every mountain and valley. These were not just promises to me; they were the foundational pillars of the house we were going to build for our souls.

The Uninvited Blessings

Life, in its extraordinary unpredictability, usually reserves the most spectacular miracles only for those moments that we believe are already flawless. The reception we attended was a river of joy, gushing with dancing, music, and clinking glasses thrown up in celebration. We were enveloped in the warmth of our family and friends, imagining that it was a day that could not hold delights. Then, the door was opened.

There wasn't a flurry of guests who walked in. There was a roar of amazement, a unified gasp that filled the room. The room, in a mix of suits and silks, was legendary. Many of India's most revered cricket stars, who were staying at the hotel to watch a match at the nearby Barabati Stadium, had been drawn by the sound and evident excitement. They arrived not as anonymous celebrities but as happy and curious guests, their stunning stature dancing with surprising grace throughout our celebration.

The expressions on my siblings' faces, avid sports enthusiasts whose childhoods were accompanied by the sound of stadiums and the whack of a bat on TV, were an incredible gift. The pure joy they expressed in the moment, their childlike excitement when they cautiously approached their idols, remains in my mind. These giants of game, these guys who had become familiar with adoring crowds, welcomed them with such genuine affection. They signed their names on wedding programs, took smiling selfies that dissolved any notion of hierarchy and shared laughter. But the real fun was the way they *became part of the wedding*. They weren't simply observers but became an integral part of the fabric. They danced to the traditional beats and shared stories that were not about fame, but about camaraderie and competition, and for only a few minutes, it was just a group of men celebrating the love of their lives.

Their presence was a powerful and unscripted symbol. It brought to mind everyone in the space that love is the most universal language. This energy can unite the many threads of human existence, the intimate as well as the famous, as well as the personal and famous, and blend the two into a single, magnificent moment of human connection. The energy they generated was not about fame. It was about the humour and joy of souls blessed with an unassuming, pure pleasure.

The Tapestry of Forever

As the evening grew darker and the stars glowed in the Bhubaneswar sky, reflected in the dazzling lights of Swosti, a profound, calm contentment settled in my heart. Srinivas's hand was my own; it was a familiar and exciting anchor. We walked around these rooms inscribed by the sound of laughter, the smells of flowers and food and the ethereal, still-inspiring wonder of a day that overshadowed every fantasy.

The Swosti Premium offered us more than just a service. It was a living, in-motion prologue. The frame was its beauty, but the work was an intense emotional work, bursting with the rich colours of tradition, the luminous light of hope, and the fantastic, dazzling streaks of serendipity. The stage was that we emerged not just as couples, but also as co-authors of a story that had just reached its most stunning beginning.

Today, many years later, as I shut my eyes, I don't see just the wedding. I feel it. The soft weight of my work, the warm hug of

Srinivas's arms after the vows, the exhilarating joy that comes from my *dhol* mixing with the euphoric whisper of a crowd in front of an athlete, and the sigh of relief at dawn that tasted like joy. These aren't memories that can be stored in a book, but rather a woven experience into the fabric of my body, to my being, into the *us* that I have created each day since.

The day I was married taught me that, even though love is born in the intimate, secluded areas of the soul, its celebrations will resonate with a force that touches the world, inviting even the most unimaginative angels to bless the occasion. The wedding we had was a vow not just to one another but to life, to life itself. We promised that our path was filled with beauty and sparkles and forever in the grand, loving arms of the incredible.

"They claim that our wedding was awe-inspiring because of legends of sport; however, the only one I can think of is the one we're creating that is a simple, timeless story of two hearts that decided to create their forever in the stunning, unimaginable and beautiful 'us' palace."

PATHWAYS OF HOPE

My key was cold inside my hands. It was a tiny brass piece that was heavier than it looked. It wasn't just a piece of metal; it was the threshold. When Srinivas put it in place with his fingers, closing my hand over it, the universe seemed to shrink to that point of contact, his warming surface against mine. And the promise encased in the cold steel. "Our primary key," the man said. His voice, usually so steady, was shaken just enough for me to feel the symphony of fear and hope playing in his soul. This tremor sounded like the introduction to our new beginnings.

The entrance to an apartment in Bhubaneswar opened with a soft, low sigh, as if the room were rising from its night of sleep to welcome us. Then there stood the plaque with the names. "Srinivas. It was his name now, ours printed in bold, simple letters. I paused and breathed deeply. It wasn't sheer beauty that captivated me; it was the simple, deep fact. His name wasn't just a signature on a letter or a caller ID on my phone. It was now anchored. It was the place where we were at home. At that point, the idea of marriage became an actual reality: an address shared and a shared journey that began at a door marked by our shared identity. A feeling of belonging, strong and still, washed over me, affirming each silent vow we made under the starry skies and whispered in the midst of crowded rooms. It was more than walls and rooms; it was a blank canvas on which we would draw our daily lives.

"Love first constructs its altar inside a new entrance in which a name transforms into an open scripture and a key transforms into more than a lock, but two hearts turn into housekeepers."

Srinivas, my beautiful and sincere Srinivas, held my hand, and his eyes were glistening with such a pure pride that my heart hurt. He took me on an excursion through empty rooms which, according to him, were decorated with fantasies. "This will be the place where we sit and read in the sun," he said, pointing towards a sunny corner. "And there, our table will be where people meet and have a good laugh until they hurt their sides." He painted on the walls, pictures of a possible future we'd only sketched out in conversation. In the empty bedroom, I was looking at him, and the distant sound of the city was the only sound. "Welcome to our Home," he whispered. It wasn't'my home.' *Our Home*. These two words, sung in a single breath, carry an eloquent pledge to be happy and companionship, of the possibility of a shared destiny, waiting to be realised within the four walls.

The subsequent weeks were a gentle dance of coexistence. Bhubaneswar was at first a city with a myriad of street names, and its echoes gradually began to mellow. It was the setting for our "firsts. The first meal we had together was a riot of spilt lentils and a rousing of slightly burned rice, served on mismatched plates, with laughter that resonated throughout the kitchen, which was still unfurnished. The laughter, which had been hesitant, eventually broke out and bounced off the walls, leaving them more vividly decorated than paint could ever do. The first argument we had, which was just a brief tussle over a topic that has since been forgotten, did not end in silence but in a deep peace that comes from reconciliation, informing us that love was not the absence of conflict but the skill of navigating it.

Then came our first celebration away from our homes since childhood. We hung lights that glowed with our nascent traditions, and the smell of our shared food offerings, a mix of my grandmother's cooking and his smoky kitchen, filled the room. This was the moment when the'rented' apartment was truly dissolving. It was *us*. It was a sanctuary in which we felt equally vulnerable and invincible, where every dawn that splashed across the floor of the linoleum seemed like a new chance waiting patiently for us to walk into.

In the following months, we travelled to Cuttack, the city that transformed him into a man that I adored. I watched as the town grew to know him. A particular turn within the river Mahanadi, A specific façade of brick and a bustling market, each one of these sights was a key opening a treasure trove of memories. A soft nostalgia swept over him, relaxing his face. "That's the place I learned to fly my first kite", the man said with his fingers pointing at a vast open field. "And the bookstore... There was a time when I spent the majority of my childhood there, imagining new worlds."

When I listened to him, it was clear that I was not just listening to stories. I was accumulating pieces of his soul. Fragments of his life that were before me, but now belong to us. It was like I was not walking through the city, but also through the stories of his life, which brought me to him. The journey through the past made our time in Bhubaneswar feel more profound. The entire outskirts of our city spoke not only of the future but also of the history that led us to where we are today. Our lives together were like a novel that was not written. Every day we flipped one page, our pen poised to create adventures in the midst of everyday life.

We were newlyweds, and our hearts were bursting with two desires: to be with each other and to build a future bigger than we. We wanted to secure our marriage not only by law and love, but also by something eternal. We looked towards the ancient soul of Odisha by embarking on a journey to Puri.

Puri was welcoming us with a ferocious, welcoming beauty, and embracing the sound of the ocean against the golden sand, and the quiet, imposing wisdom of the temples. The air was unique, filled with the traces of long-standing dedication and salt. As we held hands, we walked the streets of bustle towards the Jagannath Temple, its soaring *shikharas* reaching into the heavens. The rumble of pilgrims, priests and pigeons was an orchestra of faith. The constant rhythmic chanting that sounded like " *Jai Jagannath!*" resonated through the stones of the earth and even into our bones.

In that mystical chaos, I felt a deep connection. It wasn't only to the gods, but also to Srinivas. Our prayers of harmony, love and strength seemed to be joined by a multitude of others that were soaring upwards in the incense flame. We were just two small isolated dots in the vast world of faith, and yet, in that moment, the bond between us was strengthened and sanctified by the mass power of hope that was around us. We were a part of a stream that never ceases to flow, which was our relationship, a brand new and fresh tributary to its stream.

When we were in Bhubaneswar, we hoped to receive the blessings from the Lingaraj Temple. While Puri was a rousing tune, Lingaraj was a deeply meditative and profound poem in stone. The intricate carvings on it were more than just decorative. They were powerful narratives of gods, demons, love and war, a testimony to the passage of time. When I entered the sacred sanctuaries, there was a deep peace that fell on me, a quietness that slowed the last nervous nerves of a newlywed bride.

Srinivas, my guide again, led me through the complexities. His voice was quiet with reverence as he explained the details. "See this man here? I would often imagine stories about him when I was a kid," he confessed. Every dark corner or sun-lit artefact was a small piece of his past. While watching him share the intimate details of his past, I saw the child he was, the man he would become, all under the revered eye of the ancient temple. This temple, while displaying lasting quality and intricate detail, served as a perfect illustration of my vision for our wedding: a strong structure built with care for patients and an ever-growing devotion within.

Then we returned from these holy places not only with the ashes of our foreheads and with a calm glow in our hearts. The blessings we were seeking weren't obtained in a single significant moment, but rather in the silence we shared with God, in the squeezing of a hand in the crowd, and in the joy that radiated from his face as he opened his life to me.

Marriage, I am learning, is the most personal biography two souls could co-write. It's a daily voyage that is all its own. It's the silence that makes a day long, the laughter shared over a smoky breakfast, the willingness to show vulnerability, and the decision, every day, to turn towards one another.

Bhubaneswar is not just an urban area in an image. It is the page of our first chapter. The spiritual journey that we started at Puri and Lingaraj didn't end when they left their gates. It continues today, at our tiny altar, daily. It is through perseverance that we develop and nurture our dreams and the love we consciously choose to weave into the fabric of our lives.

The power of those old stones, the devotion that was in the chants, and the classic love stories written in the temple walls, we took the whole experience home. It's forever interwoven in the heartstrings and soul-threads from our fresh start. The story of our life is still being written, one simple, beautiful, everyday moment at a time, in this house where our name is written on the door and our love lives forever in the space of our beating hearts.

A JOURNEY OF RENEWAL

"Love isn't a single spot on a map. It is rather the return journey to it, filled with fresh ideas, old landscapes forever altered through the eyes of those who see it."

December 18th, 2018. The date is not just in my brain and on the beat of my heart. The train wheels beat a hypnotic, familiar beat against the tracks. A one that seemed like a whisper *Pune... Pune... Pune...* But this was far from a straightforward return. We were travelling backwards to advance, following the lines of our previous romance and filling it with the vibrant, overwhelming shades of our shared life. Srinivas was sitting next to me, his shoulder providing a firm, warm pressure on my own, his fingers slackly making the outline of circles across my palm. Outside, everything slowed through the past, but inside our space, time felt like a thick syrup of memories and anticipation. I watched the world change and felt my personal identity shift in tandem. I was no longer the woman who fell in love with the place; I was now a wife.

Pune was not greeted as an urban area, but rather as a real, living character in our tale. The air was thick with the smell of *jasmine* and diesel, the jumble of street vendors and rickshaws, as well as the gentle, old sound of the walls of the university; everything rushed in to greet us like a group of old acquaintances. Each street was a smooch. On this particular stretch of asphalt, the man had initially reached out to me, and his fingers were lacing with mine like he was solving a puzzle. Under the sprawling banyan tree, we had enjoyed one of our very first *Pani Puri*, and I laughed as the water's tangy taste fell down my chin. His eyes were a soft reflection of love. These paths, once witness to our secret meetings and whispered promises, are now before us not as relics but as signs of the future. They were similar, but profoundly different. They had promised us "then" then; now, they were promising us "what is next."

The transition was an amazing but terrifying vertigo. We stepped into our newly rented apartment, *the size of our* home, and the stress that came with it, a tangible reality of a life that was built, sucked my breath. We weren't reckless lovers who took weekends off. We were the creators of normal days. The love of our lives was no longer expressed in extravagant gestures, but instead in negotiating space: his bookshelf rubbing against my desk for writing, our clothes arranged in the wardrobe, and a quiet, material-based declaration of unification. The exhilaration and terror of it all would rise over me in waves as I placed dishes on the counter, fought with the shades on the curtains, or looked at the dusty mess of unpacked boxes. We were constructing a universe by hand, the heft of it all both held me and scared me.

Then, there was the stunning, intricate weaving of the family. The decision to marry Srinivas would mean to get a loving forever in the luxurious, existing clothes of his home. The uniqueness that I cherished like a shawl I had grown used to was now required to dance in the graceful and well-established patterns of their traditions. In this dance, I discovered the most unexpected source of guidance, my mother-in-law, Aarti. She didn't just welcome me, but she also curated my experience. The kitchen, which could be a refuge for foreign customs, became, under her guidance, a place of laughter and fusion.

I can remember my first unsuccessful attempt at making my family's *signature Dal*. It was thin, unseasoned, and an uninspired imitation. I sat there, in tears, weighing the weight of all expectations. Aarti Ma smiled, a sly look in her eyes. "Beta," she said her voice as hot as the morning sun, "your hands are used to munchkins of Odisha. Let us show the art of *Hing* in Maharashtra. The most delicious taste," she continued, her hands gently fixing my grip on my *spoon*, "comes not from losing the flavor of one, but rather from having them sing in harmony." At that point, she wasn't just giving me how to cook; she was giving me a philosophical approach to marriage, and for the rest of my life. The kitchen was our laboratory for alchemy. The air was sprinkled with flour, like fairy dust, while we made *chapatis*, and she told stories about Srinivas as a sly boy, bubbling along with the cooking pots. We taught her to cook the delicious kiss of my mom's *ambu and tamarind* curry, and she demonstrated to me the secrets of her perfect, fluffy *puran poli*. We weren't erasing boundaries, but instead creating an exciting, new nation between them.

My dad-in-law, Ramesh, is the silent guide in our mornings. The ritual we had was organically born as a tranquil isle in a sea of freshness. When the first light of honeyed Pune was reflected onto our dining table, we would sit together and cradle cups of chai that were steaming hot. He would sit in his seat, his eyes gazing towards a past that we only imagined. "Let me talk to you about the period," he would begin, and the world would slow down. His tales were more than tales of the past; they were stories filled with the smell of print ink as well as old papers, which he gathered from his time working at the Indian note-press. He spoke of accuracy, of the importance of confidence in creating an object that is passed through thousands of hands, of the humbleness of making the essential part of everyday life.

A few days ago, when his voice was exceptionally soft, he said, "You have to know that the idea of a brand-new note and a newlywed aren't so different. Both begin their lives fresh with potential. Both are folded, exchanged often with tenderness and sometimes rushed through without thinking. They'll bear the marks of daily life's events. The objective isn't to be perfect; however, to be significant. You must be your best, the essence of you, in every interaction and every new challenge." As I sip my tea, the profound truth of his words is buried in my soul. My fears of being accepted, about doing everything *perfectly*, were easing. He was giving me the long-term perspective, teaching me that resilience is more important than perfectionism. In his tales, I came across an old type of compass.

Through the whole thing, Srinivas. My constant. My haven in the tremendous turmoil of our growth. If the world seemed too noisy, His presence was in a quiet space. At night, if the ambiguous dynamics of a blended family made me feel unmoored, He would come to me. He didn't always provide solutions. He would instead put my arms behind me, with his chin resting on my forehead and then say nothing whatsoever. Or, sometimes, he'd just look at me from across the room, surrounded by family members, with his eyes engaged in an intimate conversation and say: I recognize you. You are mine, and I am mine, even in the midst of the chaos. The affirmations he made weren't sweeping declarations, but simple, grounded truths. A hand squeezed during an anxious meal or a note on the refrigerator. *The sound of your laughter has become my most loved sound in our home*, and the familiar, powerful words spoken before bed: "You are doing great, my dear. We're doing fantastic." He was my bridge between my former self and the present me.

There were, of course, moments of complete dissonance. A moment in which Aarti Ma's thoughtful advice regarding the organization of the pantry felt like a criticism of my very existence. I was withdrawn, nursing an inadequacy wound. In the evening, my heart racing, I went to her while she made the chai. "Ma," I ventured with my voice shaking slightly, "when you spoke about the spices... Sometimes I think I'm not doing enough of what I need." She paused, turned, and her eyes did not show offence, but instead a sudden profound acceptance. She sat down next to her kitchen bench. "Oh dear, my beautiful girl!"

she exclaimed with a smile on her lips. "When I first arrived in the house, I kept *jaggery* in a salt container for one week. My entire family was teasing me for months! I'm not trying to guide you due to your lack of. I am helping you to be guided so you don't have to suffer those *jaggery-salt* mistakes from my childhood!" The tension dissipated into a raucous, watery laugh. It was a realisation that her wisdom did not reflect my shortcomings, but rather an element of her own history that she offered to enhance the fabric of our future together.

We discovered our harmony in unimaginable gardens. After finding our love for gardening, Aarti Ma and I would sit side by side in her lush garden. My hands, as I learned about the soil, discovered an unspoken language. "This rose requires patience," she would say, and I realised she was not talking about the plant. We tended the buds and waited for the blooms to appear, and a metaphor silently unfolded between us.

Pune as a whole was our ever-changing background. The busy *Laxmi Road*, which we used to walk along and swaying around in love, became the place I learned to bargain for the freshest *Fenugreek*, with my head already planning the meal for the evening. The quiet lane behind the university was once a place for confessions of our hopes, but it was now filled with our strategies for the future. The city was our home in a peaceful double exposure: the ghosts of our youthful, passionate selves superimposed on the more solid, purposeful people we had become.

It was our first biographical sketch. It was written, not in long, sweeping pages of drama but rather in the everyday ink of shared glances, of uneasy questions that eventually grew into understanding. It was the stories told over morning tea that would become the foundation of my new self-identity. Our love story had matured. It wasn't a lonely, perfect flower. It was a sturdy and sprawling banyan tree, its roots sunk deep into the soil of families, with its branches both old and new, aiming to the sun. We returned to our canvas in Pune, and with his hands firmly balancing mine, we painted an artwork that was not merely of isolated romantic love, but of a whole life, interlocking and courageously beautiful altogether. Our return was only the beginning. The narrative of "us" was constantly written in the serene, empathetic script of a common destiny.

"Love isn't only a single spot on a map. It is rather a return journey, for it is a journey filled with new visions, the old scene forever altered through the eyes of those who see it."

December 18th, 2018. The date is not only in my mind, but also in the pace of my beat. The train wheels beat the same familiar rhythm against the tracks. A sound that sounded like whispers, *Pune... Pune... Pune...* However, this wasn't a straightforward return. We were making a backward journey to advance, following the outline of our former relationship to paint it with the intense, threatening colours of a life shared. Srinivas was next to me, his shoulders pressing firmly and warmly against mine. His fingers were silently drawing circles on my palm. Outside, the world was blurring in our secluded space, the time was thick and bubbling with anticipation and memory. I watched the world change and felt my personal identity changing with it. I was no longer the woman who fell in love with this place; I was now a wife.

Pune was not greeted as the city of Pune, but as a real, living character in our tale. The air was filled with the smell of *jasmine* and diesel, the music of rickshaws and street vendors, and the sweet, old-fashioned hum of the university walls, all coming to greet us like a choral of old acquaintances. The streets were a palempsest. On this particular stretch of asphalt, He had at first grasped my hands, his fingers laced with mine like he was solving a puzzle. In the shade of that soaring banyan tree, we'd been sharing our initial *paani puri*, and I smiled as the sweet water ran down my cheek, and his eyes were soft with sincere affection. These pathways, once witnesses to our secret conversations and whispered promises, are now available to us not as relics but as proselytes. They were identical, but they were vastly different. They had sat on our "then", and now, they had promised us "what is next."

The change was beautiful but terrifying vertigo. We entered our newly rented apartment, *the size of our* home, and the burden on top of that, the tangible reality of a life that was built, sucked my breath. We weren't reckless lovers who took weekends off. We were the creators of normal days. The romance did not exist in extravagant gestures, but rather in the negotiating of space: the bookshelf of his mate rubbing against my desk for writing as our clothes were swathed in the closet in a quiet, fabric-based declaration of our unity. The awe-inspiring excitement of all that was happening would wash over me in waves as I made dishes, fighting with the curtains' shade as I stood in the solitary, sun-drenched chaos of boxes half-packed. We were building a whole universe by hand, the weight of it all both held me and scared me.

Then there was the stunning, intricate weaving of the family. To be married to Srinivas would mean to get a loving forever in the rich, already-woven cloth of his home. My uniqueness that I had grown used to, like a shawl, was now required to dance in the graceful traditional patterns of their traditions. It was during this dance that I discovered the most unexpected source of guidance, my mother-in-law, Aarti. She didn't just welcome me, but she also curated my experience. The kitchen, which could be a secluded place of different traditions, under her guidance was a place of laughter and fusion.

I can remember my first failure to create the traditional family *daal*. It was thin, over spiced, and an uninspired imitation. I was there, close to tears, in the midst of my expectations. Aarti Ma smiled, her eyes glowing with an enigmatic glint. "Beta," she said with a voice that was as bright as the sun's morning rays, "your hands are used to the mustard seeds of Odisha. Let us show them the art of *the hing* in Maharashtra. The most delicious flavour," she continued, her hands slickly fixing my grip on the *ladle*, "comes not from not recognizing one flavour, but instead from singing with them." At that point, she wasn't just giving me a recipe; she was presenting me with the idea of marriage as a way to live, as well as to live. The kitchen was our laboratory of alchemy. Flour sprayed the air with fairy dust as we lay through *chapatis* and her tales about Srinivas as a playful boy, bubbling along with the cooking pots. She taught me the delicious kiss of my mom's *ambu tamarind* curry, and the secrets of her perfect, fluffy *puran poli*. We weren't trying to erase boundaries, but instead making a new, delicious nation between them.

The father of my children, Ramesh, is the silent guide in our mornings. The ritual we had was organically born and became a serene place in the ocean of freshness. When the first light of honeyed Pune was reflected onto our dining table, and we gathered with cups of chai that were steaming hot. He would sit in his seat, his eyes gazing at a time we couldn't even imagine. "Let me talk to you about the period," he would begin, and the world would slow down. His tales were more than stories; they were a series of parables filled with the smell of print ink as well as old papers that he had accumulated over his years working at the Indian note presses. The spoke of accuracy, of the importance of trust when creating something that goes through thousands of hands, of the humbleness involved in making vital, everyday art.

A few days ago, when his voice was very soft, he exclaimed, "You know, a fresh note and a new bride are not that different. Both are fresh and full of possibilities. Both are folded, exchanged often with tenderness and sometimes rushed through without thinking. They'll bear the marks of daily life's events. The objective isn't to be perfect but to stay significant. To be able to hold onto your value and your essence through every interaction and every new challenge." The chai I took in was a slurp, with the profound truth of his words sinking into my soul. My fears about finding my place and getting everything *perfect* were easing. He gave me the long-term perspective, demonstrating that resilience is more important than perfectionism. In his tales, I discovered an ancient type of compass.

Through the whole thing, Srinivas. My constant. My refuge in the beautiful turmoil of our growth. If the world were too noisy, his presence in a peaceful room was a relief. At night, if the ambiguous dynamics of a family that was not a single one made me feel unmoored, He would come to me. He would not always be able to offer solutions. In the end, he'd put the arms of his back around my shoulders, with his chin resting on my forehead and not say anything whatsoever. Sometimes he would just gaze at me from the room, surrounded by family members, his eyes engaged in an intimate conversation, and say, "I am seeing you." I am yours, and I am mine, right here, in the midst of everything. His affirmations weren't grand statements; they were merely steady, grounded truths. A squeezing hand at the end of the dinner table and a note scribbled on the refrigerator, *you're laughter my most loved sound in our home* or the basic powerful words spoken at night before going to sleep: "You are doing great, I love you dearly. We're doing well." He was my bridge between my previous self and my current self.

There were, naturally, moments of complete dissonance. A moment in which Aarti Ma's sincerely thought-out suggestions for organizing the pantry were interpreted as an attack on my being. I fled, shivering with an unfinished wound. In the evening, my heart racing, I walked up to her as she made the chai. "Ma," I ventured with my voice shaking slightly, "when you spoke about the spices... Sometimes I think I'm far from the things I'm supposed to be doing." She paused, turned, and her eyes were not in anger, but an instant deep appreciation. She placed her hand on the area next to her, sitting on the kitchen counter. "Oh my sweet girl!" she said, smiling on her lips. "When I first arrived in this house, I kept *jaggery* alongside salt for one week. The whole family teased me for months! I'm not guiding you due to your lack of. I am helping you to be guided so you don't have to suffer my *jaggery-salt* mistakes from my childhood!" The tension was dissolved into a raucous, watery laugh. It was a realization that her wisdom wasn't a reflection of my failing, but rather the thread from her own experience that she offered to enhance the fabric of our future together.

Our harmonies were discovered in unimaginable gardens. After finding our love for gardening, Aarti Ma and I would sit together in her beautiful garden. My hands, while learning about her soil, came up with the same language. "This rose requires patience," she would say. I could tell she was not talking about the plant. We held buds close, waiting for blooms as a metaphor for silence unfolded between us.

Pune itself was a constantly changing background. The busy *Laxmi Road*, where we would once walk hand-in-hand and swaying around in love, was the place I learned to bargain for the freshest *Fenugreek leaves*, and my thoughts were in the process of composing my evening's menu. The quiet lane behind the campus, which used to be a place for confessions of our hopes, was now filled with our concrete goals for the coming years. The city was our home in a calming double exposure, with the ghost images of our youthful, passionate selves superimposed on the more solid, purposeful people we had become.

It was our first biographical sketch. It was not written in epic sections of drama but rather in the everyday ink of exchanged glances, of uneasy questions that eventually grew into understanding. It was the stories told over morning tea that would become the basis of my new persona. Our love story was advancing. It wasn't a lonely, perfect flower. It was a sturdy, spreading banyan tree, its roots digging into the typical soil of families, its branches old and fresh, aiming towards the sun. We returned to the same canvas in Pune and, as a couple, his hand holding mine in place, we painted an artwork that was not a single love but a rich life interspersed and savagely beautiful in tandem. Our return was only the beginning. The narrative of "us" was being written daily, in the solitary emotional saga of a common destiny.

NASHIK CELEBRATION TALES

The road swung in front of us, like a silken thread pulling us towards a goal I felt in my bones. It was not just a change of place. It was the crossing of an unmarked threshold; the flip of a page that was so clear and fresh it sounded like the pressure of excitement. I left a person I knew to travel towards the woman I'd not yet met, a woman who would become his wife. The air was filled with the peaceful, magical power of beginnings. Every turn of the car's tyres sounded like a chant of *nearly there, almost her.*

In my midst, Srinivas was a constellation of unimaginable happiness. The gentle light of the fading landscape reflected in his dark eyes, which held the twinkle that I have discovered a love for the light that spoke of deep tenderness and hidden jokes. As the miles faded away, he became a storyteller and wove for me the tale of his youth in Nashik. His usually measured voice swelled with animation. He didn't speak about temples or monuments in the first place; however, he said of feelings like the flavour of the sun-warmed *ripe* fruit he bought from street vendors, the smell of the Godavari River in the morning, and the specific hue of gold the hills took during the monsoon. His memories were not just relics but alive, living things he offered to me strand by strand.

"You'll enjoy it," he promised, his voice tight with a conviction that was like a protection. His hand landed on mine, his fingers squeezing through mine, a gesture that was now our only language. However, this time it was different. It was the transfer of energy, the gentle flow of his enthusiasm, his past and his identity into my heart, waiting for him. The sensation was warm, like a breeze moving from his hand into mine, and then settling in my chest. It was like I was receiving an element of his home to hold on to, so I wouldn't be an outsider.

"He did not simply hold my hand in that moment; I was given his compass, with its needle that is forever stuck to the place his soul was the first to learn how to move."

The outside world began to change, collaborating with us in our love. The wide roads gave way to narrow roads that appeared to wrap around the contours of the earth unspoiled, lush vegetation held close, creating a lush embrace. The gentle hills, clad in deep green, were pushed aside like the sleepy bodies of ancient, gracious giants. Everywhere we turned, a new view revealed itself, a burst of red flowers against a mossy wall, the glimpse of an ethereal waterfall that looked like an elegant silver band. We opened the windows, and the breeze swung through, creating a sweet symphony. It was a fresh, spicy smell of flowers I could not remember, the rich, humid scent of freshly turned earth, and, underneath it all, the fresh, clean air from the hill. This wasn't just a leisurely trip. It was a sensory awakening and a deliberate, slow preparation for the future.

Then, Nashik revealed herself. It wasn't with a shout, but instead with the most serene, beautiful breath. In the lush greenery, the town appeared to rise from it, an ethereal extension of the natural landscape. The rumbling hum of the city's life waned into an ebb and flow of heartbeat. The peace was intoxicating, like a tangible presence affixed to the car, calming our breathing and soothing the last of my fluttering nerves in my stomach. This was the stage that was perfectly staged. The reception here would not be a mere party; it was meant to be an act of unity in the sacrament. The gentle stitching of two threads to form a single, stronger, more durable cord.

As Srinivas continued his story and stories, my excitement grew into a calm, profound appreciation. He narrated of ancient celebrations where the streets thumped with the fervour of a saint, and peaceful, modern cafés where people argued about dreams. In his tales, the tradition was not an object of contention but rather a cherished song familiar to him, and modernity was a thrilling instrument playing along. I realised then how beautifully it mirrored our own love. There was a dialogue between my uncompromising, city-spun spirit and his deeply rooted, culture-rich, thriving soul. Nashik, in its beautiful contradiction, was the incarnation of our future. It was a place where reverence and development, as well as memories and possibilities, could coexist under a sun-dappled roof.

The journey I took was the first chapter in our marriage. The goal was not the location of an outline, but the state of being. We were already beginning to enjoy the journey, the silence that we shared while watching a hawk's circle. We shared a gasp when we saw a spectacular scene, the comfort of our hands. We were not collecting distances, but moments that were each a brick inside the home we built together. At the end of the road was the celebration, a holy circle of witnesses that would see us, thank us, and forever enshrine this change by embracing the love of community and love.

The reception venue was more than just a place to be. It was an actualised promise as a dream portrayed in light, stone, and petals. As we passed through the gates that evening, with the last of the sun's rays gilding the sky, I felt like we were on the pages of a novel. Elegance is a cold term for it. It had a sensual, intoxicating appearance that could reverberate with us. In the shadows of the hills, now becoming darker, the estate was a masterpiece of harmony, the wild, unspoiled beauty of Nashik's natural landscape with a sophisticated, exquisite design. It was a symbol of that night's goal: to embrace the beauty and wildness of our love into an opulent vessel.

The entryway was a tunnel of beauty. A plethora of jasmine and marigold blossoms, strung together into elaborate *torans* and dripped down the archways, their fragrant scent is a sigh of love. The vibrant cream and saffron of the blossoms against the deep emerald-blue of the dark hills was visually striking in its contrast and harmony. We walked along a pathway lined with many Earthen lanterns, their flames dancing in the breeze like stars that were captives, creating a warm, golden glow that seemed to kiss softly on the lines of every face, smiling or saree that sparkled. The light wasn't just illuminating it; it was also blessed.

The air inside was electric, a pulsing flow of pure joy. This was an ongoing collage of sounds and feelings that radiated with crystal clear laughter when cousins got together and the warm, low murmur of older people sharing their stories across decades and the crackle of glassware, which sounded like wind chimes, the underlying theme an irresistible pulsation of music that appeared to rise from the ground and invite even the most reticent to move. This was much more than an event. The venue was not merely a backdrop, but rather a partner in making memories which I knew without doubt would be recorded in the record of my heart for the rest of my life.

On the edge of the night, my hand was once more in Srinivas's. Gratitude swelled over me. It was so powerful that it sucked the breath out of me. This beautiful gathering was a concrete affirmation. Was it the universe telling us"See? The love you feel is genuine. It's worthy of hills wrapped in darkness, and stars hanging on strings. It's an occasion to celebrate.

The moment of introduction was upon us. Srinivas's father, who was of a serene stature with eyes that held the wisdom of the gentle years, was waiting to greet me. He put a firm and friendly arm around my shoulders. He smiled, not wide but deep, extending his eyes and sculpting lines of warmth in his face. When he led me into the centre of the crowd, his voice, steady and proud, welcomed me, not just as a guest but as a family member. "This will be our baby," he said, and the word *our* resonated throughout the room, a simple, powerful word that broke down the invisible wall that stood between me and the past. Each time I shook my hands or eyes, I saw, returned not with awe, but a warm smile. Their kindness was more than mere courtesy; it was an open-armed acceptance of a growing family and a circle that would never break.

Then, amid the sea of familiar faces, Srinivas and I exchanged flowers for garlands. The ceremony is old-fashioned and is often performed in a near-ritual manner. However, for us in that dark and crowded space, it was an alchemical experience. When I lifted the thick aromatic tubes of roses and tuberoses towards him, and he did the same with me, we looked each other in the eyes. The celebration's sound diminished to a distant whisper. In that tense silence, I could feel the strength of that pledge. The flowers were not just flowers. Each flower was a vow, a vow of perseverance through the thorns of nurturing throughout the seasons, and of enduring beauty, even in the winter. We placed them over our hearts, as I sensed their weight become a tangible, anchored truth.

The whole evening was a celebration of our love story, a seamless mixture of the old and the contemporary. Traditional blessings were offered by raising our hands. The sway was a weighty reminder of the past. But the music quickly grew into a jolly, modern rhythm, and we were swept into dancing, his hands placed on my waist, and my laughter on his shoulder. It was the perfect illustration of our feet forming the new rhythm of our shared lives, as our roots drank from the same well that had once been.

"That's the night I discovered that tradition isn't an obstacle to progress; it's the soil. Love, the most ferocious and sturdiest of seeds, requires both to develop towards the sun."

As the night grew darker and the darkness grew darker, a moment of calm contemplation beckoned me. Sitting on a pillar looking out the window to watch Srinivas smile with his childhood pals, I was enthralled by the incredible contrast of a fresh start. Awe for the new path that was yet to be mapped out was a constant stream of blood in my veins, an enthralling, vibrant rhythm. However, woven into it was a gentle blue nostalgia for the girl I had been and the lonely, self-contained life I was slowly leaving behind. There was a hint of anxiety and the natural tremor one experiences when standing at an incredibly high point before the leap. There was everything in a whirling jumble of emotions.

However, as I gazed out at the Nashik night, with the mountains now solid silhouettes against the star-streaked sky and the lanterns shining their soft luminescence, I discovered the mirror of my soul. The scene was peaceful yet lively, with the chirrups of crickets and the hum of the leaves. It was quiet yet alive. It was filled with the tranquillity of the old and the glimmer of a new dawn. My inner journey was a mix of calm contentment and awe-inspiring anticipation, of a peaceful resolution, and the ever-increasing pace of excitement was evident in the surroundings. Nashik wasn't his hometown; it was now the backdrop of my growth.

The road had brought me to this moment of convergence. The road, his tales and the smell of the air, the affectionate faces as well as the dance of fire, and flowers have all been interwoven into the very first glorious page in our history. I wasn't just travelling to Nashik. With Srinivas's hands in mine, his family's love in my midst, and the holy hills as our witnesses, I had made it to Nashik. The new chapter didn't have to start. It was already in place.

MARRIAGE AND ITS TRIALS

The smell of the morning was cinnamon and pine. I still remember that vividly, the cold December morning which blew through our damaged kitchen window, bringing with it the smell of the tiny, lopsided tree we'd decorated days before. It was a concerto of hope that first morning. The sun was a soft, hopeful gold, shining down on dust motes that swayed over piles of chopped veggies and sprinkled spice containers. In that peaceful, sunlit moment, our home seemed less like a rented space and more like a living, breathing vision of a sacred, intimate space that we created by blending our wistful desires and strangled branches. I was newlywed and covered in the delicate, beautiful, dazzling mantle of that title, believing that love could create magical effects from every day.

The phone rang.

The sound was like a chunk of ice smacking against the warm space. My hand, which was squeezing knives over an unsure onion, slowed. It was Srinivas, my husband, with a lively rush of joy that was crashing into the receiver. "Wait until you know what I'm planning for you!" he exclaimed, and I could see his smile that lit up his eyes from inside. "A perfect Christmas celebration! My brother will be coming over, and we'll be heading out!"

"Out" and "Celebration ", as well as "out", floated across the sky, stunning as well as terrifying. My eyes swept across the kitchen floor before me, the soaking lentils, the rice that was measured and the unopened cookbook that I had been begging for help with. My idea was sincere and straightforward: a simple curry, a peaceful dinner, and a gentle introduction to my new role as his wife within his family a test I had carefully and frightfully set for myself.

It is essential to understand that my hands were more accustomed to the weight of books than to that of kitchen knives. My prior life was one of hostels and academics, with intellectual debates that would end at midnight, but rather than simmering sauces or the chemistry of spices. Cooking to me was not just a chore at home; it was a vast, unspoken language of love I knew nothing about. The script was changed, without my permission.

"Just let the rice go," he said, his voice wrapped in the soft gauze of assurance. "Don't worry. We'll be enjoying the evening."

The worry was like a vine that was tangled around my lungs. It wasn't just about food. It was about proving that I was a part of his world. The kitchen, which was once an area of possibility, turned into an arena. Every uncut carrot, every unreliable bit of turmeric, turned out to be an indication of my inadequacy. I spent the following hours in a trance, and the smells of cinnamon and pine now drowned out by the smell of my own anxiety.

The evening unfolded like an unusual tragedy, adorned with colourful paper. The gentle, controlled chewing was louder than any words. A calm, "The rice is... intriguing," felt like a decision. The planned excursion was the result of a blur of light and sound, over which I floated, disengaged from the ghost of my wife's failing. The excitement on Srinivas's face when he revealed to us that he had booked a table at a local jazz club, brutally, with the dread sinking in my heart. I was a character in a play that was not my own, and I was smiling as my heart broke.

Then the criticism like these things goes, travels. It landed on his mother. The call came on the 26th day, an evening when the home's silence was complete, without the echoes of the day's devastation.

"Beta," her voice typically warm, was measured with a scalpel of soft touch. "Cooking for someone else is one of the main expressions of love. It's the way we express our love for someone without speaking."

The line of conversation hummed between us, a harbinger of a truth about culture that, at the moment, like the stipulations of a life sentence. Her words didn't judge me, but they pierced deeper than any knife I have in my kitchen. They revealed a terrifying problem: my inability to navigate my kitchen was translated into this ancient yet powerful dialect, into a failure to love. The gap remained unresolved and threatened to rip a hole in the foundation of our brand-new relationship. The celebrations were not only a smackdown against an internal struggle, but were sucked into it.

In the sweltering days that came, a cold space stood between Srinivas and me. It wasn't a battle or a storm; it was a peaceful frost. He perceived my grief as a reaction that was too strong; I thought his enthusiasm was an expression of disapproval. We spoke about different emotions in different ways. In the moment I asked to know the source of my anxiety, he provided an optimistic solution: "We'll take your order at a later moment!" not realising that, for me, I didn't have a "next date," only the echoing in success of this moment.

I felt shackled by the unspoken expectations that we each brought into our marriage. I had made it clear to him about my lack of culinary knowledge, but he was a slave to an unspoken assumption that love would naturally incite the ability. I had made my own notion that my passion for food, in its most pure academic form, was sufficient. Both of us were wrong.

Our silence showed me the awe-inspiring number of unspoken words. I realised that the communication between us was not only about words, but also about the fear that lies beneath the complaint, and the necessity that lies beneath the silence. When I was at home, one night, as I stared at the blank screen of my television, I finally asked him the question, not "What's going on?" but "What does it feel like in your heart the moment you think about the food you'll cook for people?"

The problem was turning the key in the lock. It was an invitation, not for solving, but to observe. The dam was broken. I talked about the invisible chains, the performance anxiety, as well as the anxiety of being judged by a rubric I'd never received. He listened with a sincere interest, and his initial confusion morphed into a painful knowing. He admitted his own private stress to display his beautiful marriage and to connect my world to his.

"We constructed our house out of dreams, but we forgot to plan to deal with storms," I would write later. This was the reality. We were loved and the solid timber; however, we were not equipped to withstand the rumbles.

The Christmas we had to endure the first time turned out to be our unreliable teacher. The experience taught me that resiliency is not an inflexible refusal to give up or break, but the soft, daily determination to bend and change. It was not surrender; it was the imaginative constant act of creating a common language. We slowly started making our own plans. He would sit with me in my kitchen, but not as a food critic, but as a fellow adventurer, sharing stories of burnt and charred rotis. I would talk to him about the writers I adored and weave my personal history in the fabric of our lives. We made places for 'I' inside the 'we.'

I also sought out my inner peace. The chaos of merging lives and balancing an intense personal ambition with a new family demanded an inner anchor. I found it unexpectedly in the utter silence of the Vipassana meditation retreat. For 10 days of silence, I faced the fear that was brewing within me. I recognised my anxiety was not a frightened monster but rather a fearful part of me that I had never embraced. I was able to see the waves of anxiety without being swept away by the raging waters. I returned to him with a brand-new rulebook, but with a newfound calmness and a centre from which I could be engaged, enjoy, and, yes, learn to cook from a place of choice without fear.

The trip to his home with family members was slower as it was a delicate dance of respect and gentle redefining. I learned how to write his mother's signature, not for the sake of submission, but as a love note in a language she loved. In turn, I wrote mine in books, in conversations with my colleagues about my work. As time passed, the story began to shift. I wasn't the wife who couldn't cook, but my wife, who was learning, who brought various kinds of wealth to the dinner table.

As I look back, I see that the real beauty of that awful, beautiful initial Christmas came from the slit that it created in our perfect dream. By it all, the intricate, amazing process of marriage could begin. We discovered that a perfect marriage isn't an ideal union, but rather a loving, respectable parallax of two distinct orbits which form a right angle, creating a single beautiful, gorgeous star.

"Love isn't just the foundation you built once in your life," I now know, "but the sanctuary you build each room each time you weather its wall."

The first day of December, I was convinced that the scent of cinnamon and pine was the best way to greet the new year. I was mistaken. The promise was found in the struggle, in the tears shed over spilt rice, in the hard-fought conversations in the darkness, and in the choice to create something completely personal from the beautiful and broken pieces of our own tradition and self. Our story has become a testament not to a romance that was perfect from the beginning; however, it was an uncompromising love that was strong enough to begin with and grow into.

143

CHARTING NEW HORIZONS

Human hearts are an enthralling cartographer. It does not draw its maps using ink, but instead in the slender, silver scratches of memories as well as the vivid bleeding colours of hope. My map at the beginning of 2019 was an untruth. One page displayed the rugged, thrilling coast of a future that I had imagined with Srinivas, an era filled with foreign markets that smelled of spices and rain, as well as lost conversations that we didn't know, of a passion that was our only real guide. The other page displayed a neat, grid-like town that was a place of duty, a city of the soul in which every street was named after the duty of its owners and each house was the design of another's expectations. On New Year's Day, I stood at the juncture between the two worlds, and the gulf in me resonated with a silence more profound than any other sound.

The New Year's Eve celebration at our house, which used to be a place for private laughter, was now turned into an eerily silent stage of appraisal. Srinivas's mother, a lady who was awe-inspiring in her grace and in her unspoken rules, had come to stay with us. Her presence wasn't a shadow, but rather a shift in the atmosphere itself; it was a change from the warm, hazy illumination of intimacy to a swathe of harsh, threatening spotlights. The sound of champagne glasses was not like a celebration, but more like an unintentional toast to a future she imagined. Her watchful eyes, tender but uncompromising, traced the script of our lives. I could feel both of us, Srinivas and I, struggling with lines we'd not practised.

I can remember being with him at the table we shared and the spectre of the event lingering in my mind like an aroma. Our silence was an unwelcome, entirely new guest. It was then that I realised with a force that strained my throat, how quickly the currency of our love had altered. We no longer traded in the shiny coins of our dreams of renting a house in the Scottish Highlands or volunteering on a Thai beach, but rather in the real-world paper notes of bank bills, career trajectories, and the family's smiles. The flame that once raged was not gone, but it wasn't. However, it was stored and covered with the heavy and necessary ashes of adulthood. It was warm; however, we were no longer all right.

"Love is a beautiful thing. It's first spring, proclaims its hopes toward the skies. However, to make it through winter, it needs to learn to speak the sacred language of whispers from the roots."

My profession was the first tangible evidence of our pact. Marketing was my love, a field where creativity and connection abound. It was like a continuation of my voice. But the pragmatic voice of my father, an individual who valued stability above all else, rationally recommended Human Resources. "It is secure, respected, with a clear path," said the man. And, in his explanation, I could hear the echo of hundreds of unspoken concerns regarding our safety and our future family. Our responsibilities. The shift from HR to marketing was far more than a change in business cards. It was the delicate removal of a portion of my personal map and the acquiescence of a more functional one. This was the first significant sacrifice as a couple, as a down payment on the shared life being developed by many hands.

Our bond began to show the gentle, aching signs of the pressure. Eyes that were once positioned across the space in a conglomeration of joy have now frequently disappeared, filled with conversations that were too turbulent even to begin. A glance missed at a gathering or a silent sigh over the food, these tiny absences created a void between us. The grand gestures of romance from our early days of surprise excursions, the poetry written on pillows were swept away like a wave and left behind a scene of a quiet life, like him fixing the leaky tap, without asking for it and me ironing his shirt to attend the important event. These were also love letters; however, they were written with a sluggish, tired pencil rather than the vibrant ink used before.

The decision to travel to Igatpuri to participate in the 10-day Vipassana retreat stemmed from this solitary, desperate feeling. It wasn't an escape, but rather a profound confrontation. I had to get away from the roar of voices that his family, society, the frantic scream of my heart's achingly broken, and listen to the voice of my own, if it was still there, my own. The promise of peace was not a sigh but a shivering silence. When I put my basic bag, I was left with bitterness upon my lips. I was seeking myself in a meditation centre because I felt like an outsider in my own home, in my own personal love story.

The road trip there was a journey through my own frenzied emotions. Each mile between me and our apartment, from the burden of that loving love, I was shivering with a combination of guilt and happiness. The guilt of leaving, wanting to be alone from the life I'd chosen. A sense of relief for the brief respite from the responsibilities. I was a wife, a daughter-in-law, and a potential HR professional, but who was *I*? The woman who longed for the scent that arose from the Cambodian rain? Or the one who diligently created employee handbooks?

The first few days at the centre felt like torture of the soul. The opulent silence, intended to pull one inwards, only amplified the sonic roar within my head. I was sitting cross-legged on my mat, and in my closed eyes, I couldn't find peace. I could see Srinivas's face not the way it appeared at the moment, sluggish and exhausted; however, it was as it was on our first visit to

Hampi with him: sunburned, smiling, singing a silly song in the roar of the motorbike we had hired. I could feel that glimmer of his hands in my hand, not the short comforting squeeze of the last few months, but the ferocious grasp of a man who was leading me into a thrilling adventure. These memories reverberated so clearly, they were pains, sharp and gorgeous.

Vipassana helps you observe sensations without reactivity. The ability to let pain rise to a peak, then disappear. While I practised sitting in the pain of my legs, I started to feel the emotional pain that was raging in my heart. I felt the intense sting of resentment toward the career I had lost and the home I had left behind. I felt the dull ache of anxiety that the person I loved the most, and I, were now becoming friendly roommates. I felt the clinging, nostalgic warmth and its dangers. I let them all flow across me. They did not appear as truths but as sensations. And, in the midst of the storm, a clarity grew.

The love wasn't gone. It was laid to rest. We'd mistaken creating a new life for the purpose of defending the position. We'd been so busy building the furniture for a prestigious future that we'd neglected to allow our souls to move. Travel and culture weren't flimsy. They were the only way of
communicating *our* affection. When we shut them down, we had cut off the most essential communication channel.

Seven days later, during a meditation walk on a gravel path, the realisation did not come in a scream, but rather as a calm knowledge. ***"A compromise that extinguishes the core light of each person is not a foundation, but a burial."*** I was at the mercy of my personal light and, in doing so, I had been soliciting Srinivas to become ghosts. True partnership shouldn't entail the two of us turning into smaller, less luminous versions of ourselves to suit an external design. It was necessary to create an entirely new look that reflected our vibrant, original souls *in addition to* our new obligations.

On the final day, as the peaceful silence broke, the world seemed distinct. The birds' chirps were not just noise; they were an actual song. My voice, as I thanked the teacher, was familiar to me. I returned to my home without an agenda, but rather with the nexus of truth.

I stumbled across Srinivas inside our home, the one that felt like a stage. He leaned forward, and it was the first time in many months that our eyes met and were held. It was not in a way of avoiding each other, however, but in a gesture of genuine, unaffected acknowledgement. The silence that we had now was not void, but charged as the air in the monsoon.

"I missed you," the man's voice was rough. The dam fell. The dam was broken not by accusations but by confessions. He spoke about the stress he felt and the guilt of watching my heart wane beneath the well-meaning plans of his family. He admitted that he, too, missed the man who had a dream of Moroccan evenings and sunsets, as did I. "I feel like I'm managing a merger," the man said, looking sad, "instead of nurturing a marriage."

We talked the whole night. We wept. It was hilarious the whole thing. We didn't make any big choices at the time; however, we did the most radical thing we've done in recent times: we introduced our real personas to each other. I talked about marketing not as a dream tossed aside, but as a real part of my life. He told me about his father's fears, and his desire to protect us has morphed into a stifling.

The road back to each of our partners was slower and more deliberate than our first fall. There were difficult conversations with his parents. Srinivas was the one to lead in a firm, but warm, telling us that to allow our spurgeoning marriage to develop, it required the sun of our own hopes. This involved me writing an idea for the hybrid position that blends HR structure and marketing expertise, an intersection of my passion and practicality.

The most important thing was us taking back our own language. We put a giant world map on the wall in our bedroom. In one corner, we drew our financial goals for the next five years and the grid that defines our obligations. In the other, we began writing down places we'd like to visit with vibrant red pins, not in the near future, with dates drawn on top. A long weekend in Sri Lanka. A savings plan for Iceland. The map became the ideal illustration of our relationship, rooted in the soil of our home yet always striving to explore new horizons.

The burden of expectations was never completely gone; however, we were able to construct a shared house beneath it, one that we had designed for ourselves. The house began to look like a home once more, not a perfect, static stage, but rather a lively, messy, sometimes messy workspace where two people were creating the kind of life that honoured both their roots and the wings they were flying.

The New Year that started with so much tension and uncertainty ended up giving us the most precious gift of all: confidence to explore our own paths, in tandem. We discovered that love isn't just a static picture to be enjoyed and admired, but a living, moving landscape that requires continuous sharing of the map. The most stunning places can't be found on a single map, but rather in the unexplored, sacred space of two hearts that aren't willing to give up on the other.

WHISPERS OF LOVE

A Personal Note Before We Begin...

"Love is not a number on calendars, but rather the ink that we use to record our lives. Sometimes it flows in elegant script, but at times, it spills across the page, leaving a messy, beautiful testimony of a shared life." A selection of my journals, 15 February.

The air is shifted in February. It's not just cold, but also a particular *tightening* all over the globe, a collective inhalation in millions of chests. My experience of the very first sight of crimson in the window of a store and the very first sweet advertisement for diamonds has always brought a familiar twin stream of blood through my veins. It's a thrilling excitement immediately anchored by the hefty weight of anticipation. Valentine's Day. A day that promises exquisite poetry of love, yet often delivers the unpredictability of human weakness.

I've always loved romance. The kind that isn't naive and is a believer in a perfect, fairytale conclusion, but the genuine kind that believes in the holy, nitty, beautiful work of selecting one person day in and day out. My love, my Srinivas, is a man with quiet depths and unwavering dedication. Our story of love was not one of lightning bolts, but instead of an unhurried, steady sunrise, the kind that slowly warms your heart until you're bathed in bright, golden light. We constructed a universe in our apartment with mismatched mugs and the blanket that we always struggled over. It was a world I loved.

However, as February began each year, a small crack would appear in the heavenly cosmos. The outside world would encroach with its booming roar on what love *ought to* appear like: magnificent gestures, exquisite diamonds, well-planned moments of joy. It was a tangible thing. It sat in the middle of us and breakfast, and was a silent third person reading the paper. I would look at Srinivas, my kind engineer, who was pragmatic and showed a slight fear as he read the restaurant reviews. He wanted to present me with the moon because everyone was screaming it was the only thing that could be considered a worthy offering. Then I, too, began to spiral into a trance, pondering whether my gift or my choice of words could be enough to convey the vast ocean of my feelings to him in one meaningful day.

The city was transformed into a stage for this epic show. Streets transformed into tunnels were filled with pink foil and red velvet. The florists' windows were shrines to roses, with each flowering stem a silent reminder of a dedication that was less than perfect. The chocolates' creations sounded like a chant of sensual pleasure, a taste that the real world, with its bills and fatigued evenings, cannot beat. The external celebration, intended to celebrate love, often felt like a measuring stick against which our everyday, deep, intimate love was found wanting.

In the midst of it all, hummed the unstoppable engine of modern-day life. My new job as a recruiter at the teeming start-up was a beast, with its appetites unpredictable. It was not a fan of dates with romantic significance. It required late nights or urgent phone calls, and an unending flow of persuasion. The mythical balance "work-life equilibrium" everyone lectures about was like balancing dumbbells and diamonds at the same time. One demanded careful, concentrated attention and the other exhausting endurance. To lose either of them was to risk shattering something valuable or crushing something important. My affection for Srinivas is my diamond. My job was to carry the weight I had to take to create a future I was confident in for all of us. The stress of holding both of us was the unspoken music of our lives.

The steadfast love I have discovered is not as a separate entity, unaffected by the whirlwinds that afflict the globe. It's not a peaceful, calm pond. It is a deep, tough tree that develops *due to* the events, its roots stretching and becoming immersed in the earth as it withstands each blow. Our tree has been through the elements before, with doubts about career, as well as personal losses, and the gratifying, straightforward tension of two separate lives blending. We have always nurtured development from these. However, the storms that I didn't quite know how to handle were those that swept in from the loving, well-intentioned coastlines that our families extended.

Family. The word itself is a tapestry, made with threads of unshakeable support, and sometimes accidental constraint. These are the people who tell our stories as well as our cheerleaders. They carry the wisdom of centuries and the weight of a generation. Their expectations for us are based on affection. Still, they also form expectations that are like moulds we need to be squeezed into, usually leaving some of us with bruised, hurting, private, individual, particular parts.

The tensions boiled to the surface the night before, but not in February, but during the tense preamble. A minor disagreement about holiday plans, an insignificant issue, grew into a tired discussion. We were going through the familiar logic, exhausted and rooted in it, when his brother, who was visiting for the weekend, decided to intervene. He was a presence typically a source of laughter and camaraderie, but suddenly he was an inspiration.

"Well, *I* think," Srinivas said while leaning toward the future, his tone reminiscent of that of a mediator who has already decided on a side, "that Srinivas has a concern about the family obligations. You must look at the larger picture."

The room shook. The argument wasn't just ours anymore in the private room where we cleaned. A window had been left open, allowing for commentary from outside. Srinivas, in search of solidarity or perhaps a solution to the stalemate, didn't simply close the window. The draft was let through. His brother's words, meant to provide advice, turned out to be salt on a wound that I had not fully recognized existed. They illustrated how families, seated at their rings, could inadvertently fuel an unintentional small fire that can turn a spark of discord into a perceived alliance and deceit. I felt ganged up on. Isolated. It was a lonely feeling "We" of our marriage quickly became divided into "you and your family" and "me." The emotional strength required in that moment was Herculean. It wasn't about winning an argument about travel; it was about safeguarding the sacredness of our private lives from an ill-intentioned attack.

The next day, the cavalry rolled in. The parents of Srinivas, who had heard the whispers of discord, gathered in to "mediate." Their love was sincere, their wish to bring us all together. However, their presence hung like a weight. It was not two individuals trying to communicate with each other. We were performing on stage, tasked with showing "marital harmony" to a worried public. The tension to present a harmonious and peaceful front was overwhelming, which stifled the honesty and honest communications we had to *achieve* that harmony. We spoke in shrewd and diplomatic phrases, our eyes shut to the pain. We cultivated their notion of a partnership, but in my mind, my personal relationship with Srinivas was struggling under the pressure of external scrutiny. It was a feeling of profound loneliness to be alone in solitude while sitting alongside the person you love dearly.

It is in this crucible that emotional resilience is formed. It's the quiet inner steel that enables you to accept criticism from your partner or a sibling, or even a parent, and not let it affect you. It's having the courage to face the pressure of expectations without letting it destroy your personal, authentic self. It's holding on to your freedom from the "I" that you were and are still when you are adamantly nurturing "we. "We." That evening, after they had left the room, the silence between Srinivas and me did not feel tranquil. It was the quiet of a battlefield following the troops' having left in a haze of unexploded ordnance and unspoken things.

Then, Valentine's Day arrived.

My plan had been poetic. I had planned to leave work early to turn our living space into a tranquil grotto with gentle lighting and his most loved music, and then cook a lavish meal he was a fan of, but which I didn't have time to cook. It was my big gesture, my way of atoning for the tensions of recent times as well as proof that, despite the world, family, and the chaotic start-up, *he* was my focal point.

However, life, with its brutal realism, does not sway to poetry. A crucial negotiation was placed on a knife-edge and demanded my attention. Every moment I was at my computer, writing convincing letters, seemed like a crime. The intimate, vibrant evening I had envisioned started to fade like a painter's sketch under the rain. My clock was my torturer. When I snatched my coat, the city was filled with a chorus of happy couples. The laughter provided a striking contrast to the panic rumbling in my throat.

I returned home late, my arms were not loaded with gourmet food items; however, they were stuffed with dry cleaners I'd rushed to collect, as well as a faded, overpriced arrangement from the one corner store still in business. The house was dark. It was a harrowing moment when I thought he'd lost hope. Then I noticed the soft light emanating in the dining room.

Srinivas was there. He did not express anger, but rather a peaceful, sluggish patience that pierced me more than any criticism. The table was set. Takeout containers, still warm, were put next to two lit candles. The simple, familiar image was an eerie, savage contrast to the dreamlike vision I had vowed myself.

"I... I... negotiations... The negotiation... sorry, I really wanted to ..." My words fell apart and were sucked away by the intense pressure of tears. It was the climax of all that had happened: the burden of the Christmas season, the stress on my shoulders at work, the unresolved pain from the family feud, and the crushing loss of my expectations. I wasn't just in the wrong place for dinner. I felt like I hadn't done enough to fulfil the concept of the day, and in turn, I failed to show him the extent of my affection.

He didn't approach me at once. He stared at me, and really did, looking past my frazzled hair and professional clothes, and into the exhausted, utter *desire* in my eyes.

"Come and sit," he said in a soft voice. "You're here now."

Then the thing broke and was rebuilt. When I poured out the angst of my day, the constant demands of a start-up, as well as the guilt and pressure I placed on myself, He took note. He did not listen as a judge but as my friend. And I realized my horrendous mistake. In my search for the "perfect" Valentine's gesture, I had omitted the fundamentals of understanding.

The art of understanding in marriage isn't just knowing that he drinks his coffee black or dreads hearing the sound of metal being scrubbed. It's the constant, active effort to recognise the weight your spouse is carrying. My tardiness wasn't due to poor time management; it was the image of a woman trying to establish a career in a volatile world, building an even stronger foundation for a better *future*. His takeaway meal was not an ineffective effort; it was a declaration of determination. It stated, "The world is chaotic, and I'm here waiting. Our peace isn't in the air; it's here, right with us."

The night we went to bed, with some lukewarm takeout and a beautiful, sad bouquet, it was not an enthralling, romantic storybook romance. We were able to have something more. We made peace with the world's expectations. We started the real, messy, beautiful work of stitching our universe together, not with an elaborate thread, but with the more durable fibre of shared reality and a tolerant grace.

It was Valentine's Day that I had thought of as a performance; it turned out to be the day we chose instead just to be present to the complex, amazing reality of our lives. What I came to realize, and realized it was probably the most beautiful thing of all.

A HEARTFELT AWAKENING

5 March, 2019, dawned with standard shades of gold and grey. I can remember the particular lighting that flickered across the bamboo blinds, stripping our rumpled sheets. I recall the familiar smell of dark-roast coffee being brewed at the stove, and the distant symphony of Chennai's morning traffic, a sound so constant it became silent. Nothing was threatening to be heard, no feeling of dread. It was a Tuesday. Like any other Tuesday, one, or so I thought.

My Srinivas moved his shadow on the window as he pulled on his crisp white shirt. I watched, just as I have done many times before, how his fingers tinkled, steadily tightening every button my dreamer, my artist, whose laughter could shake all the wall surfaces of our small home. In recent times, this laughter was interrupted by a distinct sound, which was a dry and persistent cough, which he brushed away with a wiggle of his hand. "It's the city dust, *jaanu*," the man would tell me, while kissing my forehead. "Or perhaps your love, stuck in my throat." The way he breathed was also fast and shallow, like a bird that had become frantic and was trapped in his chest; however, he believed it was due to his "bustle of life." We were both adept at crafting narratives to drown out the screams of our frail bodies.

The next morning, however, an uneasy insistence arose in my chest. It wasn't an expression of fear, at least not yet. The reason was the wife's hard-working love, a force often expressed as gentle or nagging. "Your annual check-up," I reminded him, and handed him a cup of coffee. "At Thyrocare. Today. There are no excuses." He groaned with a boyish tone, but his eyes matched mine, and he spotted what I'd drawn. He sighed. It was a common choice, triggered by a cough and my wife's worry. We didn't realise we were crossing to the other side of our previous existence.

The hospital was a laboratory in the sterile state of calm. The air was scented of antiseptic and calm anxiety. I was in the waiting area reading glossy magazines, and the words were blurred. The time slowed and dwindled. As Srinivas was seen from the shadows, his face was an unnatural canvas, and his eyes, these dark, expressive pools I had spent fifteen years swimming in, were shaking. "All done," he stated in a way that was too bright. The doctor had accelerated specific tests because of the symptoms. We were told to wait.

The report did not arrive with a dazzling explosion; instead, it was a soft, deadly sound as a printed sheet landed on the desk. The world didn't break, but it disintegrated in the corners, disappearing until the only thing visible in sharp, frightening in the spotlight were words printed on the page: Abnormal Lipid Profile severely Elevated Cholesterol. Risk Factors include: High. Medical terminology black and white, and yet it was screaming in the colour I'd not seen before. It was the colour of imminent loss.

I gazed at my energetic and loving husband. He was the man who could argue philosophical topics with tension, the man who could draw sunsets with his words, and who was my hands, like it was the most valuable artifact. This paper said his very lifeblood, that inner river was dripping, and becoming hostile to his back. It was a quiet, profound, clinical quake. The foundation beneath our future that I believed was bedrock proved to be sand.

The return trip was a trip through a sombre world. The vibrant bustle of the city seemed to slow, as if viewed through thick glass. He sat in at the windows, his face as a statue of reflection. I grasped the steering wheel with my white knuckles. Every beat of my heart was a shout of prayer. This was the moment we woke up unexpectedly and violently. It is vulnerability not as an abstract idea, but rather as a tangible, cold presence in the passenger seat in front of us.

The evening was draped over our house. The calming shadows were different. They were a haven for our anxiety. We sat on the small balcony, watching the sky bleed from violet to orange. We sat in silence, thick-filled with unspoken thoughts. I was scared to speak, to add an expression to the frightening thoughts that flooded my mind.

He then turned his attention towards me. A final ray of evening light stung his eyes, but not in the usual spark of play but with a raw steel that was forged. He reached out to me with a touch that was familiar and a little frantic. His voice, as it came, was unrestrained, stripped of its poetic sound, and reduced to a fundamental reality.

"I have been a fool," the man said in a tone that was not saturated with self-pity but carved from regret. "I have been painting on a canvas that was rotting from behind." He was looking at his intertwined fingers before turning his gaze to mine, his gaze holding me in the moment with a fervour that held me. "I must change. Not for a physician. Not for a doctor's report. I must make a change to suit us. To be able to change for the "us" that has not yet arrived."

The air escaped my lungs. The event was much more than just a promise; it was a beginning. In that statement *to us* was the blueprint for an entirely new world. It was a recognition that his body wasn't solely his; it was the vessel for our dreams and shared goals and the place for my soul. Reducing alcohol consumption, embracing exercise, and changing an entire lifestyle of habits weren't on a list of clinical tasks. They were holy vows that he made, bricks he pledged to build for a future that he believed we could have.

In my journal that night, I made the following note: "Love doesn't just mean a blossoming vine. It is also diligent, regular care of the roots, particularly when you notice they're not well. This morning, I was reminded that my husband made a promise to care for his roots, as their health is crucial to the life of our entire beautiful garden."

The next phase wasn't a dramatic montage; it was a peaceful change in the routine. Our promises were part of the weft and warp in our everyday tapestry. Afternoon whisky glasses were replaced by long walks during which our conversations were no longer a whirlwind of the minutiae of our day, but went deeper. We discussed fears we'd put aside, hopes we'd dismissed as unattainable, and the simple, deep gratitude for the sunset we shared.

Cooking was a form of communal creation and not just a source of food. We mastered the language of nutrition and transformed our kitchen into an apothecary for affection. I could see the struggle on his face as he picked up the second serving of rice with ghee, and the smile of pride that lit up when he picked up an apple bowl. Every choice was a quiet love note. The man who was once mostly in the realms of thoughts was now ferociously and fervently committed to the physical body as his temple being.

The health issue he was suffering from was a brutal editor who cut away all non-essential. We had to stop *and take* moments to commemorate special occasions. A glass of tea in the garden was the perfect occasion for a celebration. The sudden rain of the afternoon was a good excuse to put on the music and dance in the living room. He held his breath, which was still faster than it should be, shivering around my neck. "We are making memories of awareness," the man said at times, his lips pressing against my temple. "Every conscious breath is a new heirloom."

We came across a profound paradox. When we acknowledged our vulnerability, we constructed a wall. The fact that he admitted his fear didn't make him weak to me; it made him a person, one who was able to touch and was inexhaustibly courageous. My anxiety about losing him, previously a silent spectre when I spoke to him, lost some of its strength and became a burden shared by all that was halved in weight.

A few nights ago, during an intense monsoon storm, he admitted, "I do not fear dying, *jaanu*. I'm afraid our relationship will be cut short. I am scared of painting, I'll never be able to paint close by." The brutal honesty of the situation shattered my world and made me come back and more resilient. My own tears poured out not only from a sense of anxiety, but also from the overwhelming honour of being so interwoven with another's.

This flaw transformed into the most personal language we have ever spoken. It took away the dirt of petty frustrations and unspoken anger. When you've stood at the top of a cliff and gazed down, even the most minor bumps on the road aren't noticed. The way we communicated became gentler and more patient, infused with an omnipresent sense of empathy. We weren't just spouses and husbands and comrades-in-arms in a fight for a common tomorrow.

The experiences showed us how love isn't an inert object; it is an ever-changing, living entity. The passionate, heady passion of our youth was gorgeous and wild. But the new love we formed in the fiery crucible of commitment and fear was something else. It was a warm, long-lasting shine. It wasn't about dazzling heights; it was more concerned with providing solid, unchanging ground.

The word "love" we have learned is a verb that requires the present participle. It is *selecting, nurturing, listening, and fighting for*. It's showing up not only when music is on, but when it is quiet. The rewards of this kind of relationship aren't merely joy, but something much more sturdy and profound: a deep joy grounded in simple love, a strength that can withstand turbulence, and a relationship like a perfect refuge.

Rediscovering love in the midst of struggle did more than strengthen our bond; it changed it. We treasured not in huge, extravagant gestures, but in tiny details like the constant rhythm of his heartbeat beneath my ear when we embraced his shoulders, the serene determination in his eyes when he put on his running shoes, and the peaceful weight of his hand against my thigh while we lay in bed.

As I type this post, Srinivas is in the room to his left, singing an old Ilaiyaraaja song. His breathing is more relaxed, and he is enjoying a peaceful tide. Recent reports indicate an improvement in his health, with his numbers bending to the will of his determination. However, the real change isn't only through his bloodwork.

The story we tell is not a fairytale of an issue solved. It's a love biography written in the language of vulnerability and secured by a commitment. The storm that hit us on 5 March did not destroy us. It cleared the air and left everything with an astonishing beautiful clarity.

We live our lives with a delicate awareness, a romantic view through the prism of second opportunities. The love story we have been told continues, but not in a childish illusion of endless ease; instead, as a conscious, daily work we're painting together, stroke by carefully loving stroke, on a canvas we are aware of as stunningly beautiful and devastatingly fragile. That knowledge makes each colour we choose to paint together ever more vibrant.

"They claim that the force of storms tests the most sturdy buildings. I had no idea that this was true of hearts. Ours was not able to endure the raging winds, but it discovered, through the roaring breeze, a fresh and better method of beating."

SHADOWS AND NEW BEGINNINGS

Within every household, there's an unspoken structure that's an invisible network of expectations on which our life is suspended. It's not just concerned with love but also about legacy; not only affection and appearance, but also. We are born with these codes that are not spoken, gentle yet strict pressures that influence our choices, careers, and even our heartbeat. In the Srinivas family, this code was interwoven with threads of respect, integrity, and a deep-seated sense of pride in their namesake, passed down through generations as a meticulously refined family heirloom. We believed in this system, my love and I. We thought that it was what kept us all together. Then we learned that the most significant strength isn't in the image itself but in the beautiful, desperate bond between two people, even when the image breaks.

The story we tell is. Not just a narrative of betrayal, but rather a story of a love affair that was compelled to establish roots in the cracked earth. It tells the story of how we came to realise that the most glorious dawns often follow the darkest, starless night.

If I could identify the exact moment when the planet was tilted to the left, it would be on April 10. The day began as every other, soaked in the everyday smell of coffee in the morning and the soothing, familiar sounds of a life shared. In the evening, the date had turned into an inscription in the date book, a pre- and postmark in the history of our family.

The disclosure of Srinivas's brother's deeds didn't just pop up in our lives. It exploded among the people. The news came as a stinging blow, a sucker punch to the heart that left us longing for the breath of normalcy. I can recall the exact nature of the silence following Srinivas's quiet phone call. It was a thick, suffocating silence, like a smothering of the familiar sounds we heard in our home. The clock was ticking louder and louder, with each *tick* an accusation. The world outside continued to rage, a gruesome scene of indifference.

My first reaction was stupefying, white-hot disbelief. *What?* The question was an insect, racing against my brain's glass. What could someone in the same fabric of our lives and who had the same past as well as the same blood and laughter at the table, defy the very values that the fabric was intended to symbolise? The man I knew was friendly, fun, and a loving brother and son. The choices he made now painted a stranger's image, while the psychological dissonance became emotional pain.

And then, I gazed at Srinivas.

My love is my anchor. I watched the storm strike him. It was the gradual slump of his shoulders, as if an invisible leaden weight was placed on them. It was evident in the way the light disappeared from his eyes, leaving an unadulterated landscape. Unadulterated pain. The pain did not simply sit *on* the person; it had settled *in* the man, altering the way he acted. His voice, which is usually comfortable and confident, changed into an unrecognisable ghost as it was beguiled by a deep tremor that shook him to sadness. He walked around our home like a man in a dream, touching familiar objects such as the seat back or the inside of the book, as an attempt to confirm their realness in the world that had abruptly changed into a fantasy.

This was the very first test for *our love for one another*. Our affection, once an enclave of comfort and a haven, was exposed on the cliff's edge, being tossed by the wind of fear and dismay. Two souls trapped in an unsettling lifeboat in the middle of the sea, and the only option was to row with each other or be taken in by the sea in its entirety. In those first rough days when we had to learn to speak in a different language, that was a language of long silences, held in tightly interlaced hands, and of tears washed away with no words but by the gentle pressure of the cheek against a shaken back. We were on the edge of a storm, and our love became both the vessel and compass.

The dishonour, as all things can be, was unable to be kept in check. The stain spread, cold and persistent, across every corner of the home of the family, and through every link. The most tragic victim is his family. Watching the pillars of your life fall away is an unimaginable pain. His proud father's appearance diminished, and a film of ungushing tears and awed guilt constantly obscured his mother's bright eyes. The unanswered question hung in the air among them. It was a hefty cloud of mist: *Where did we get it in the wrong direction?* They grappled not just with their son's actions but also with their own lifetime of assumptions that had become invalid.

The brother's decision to leave the family and find a haven in a PG place of residence was a seismic shift. This act created a gap. Gatherings with family, once lively orchestras of stories that merged and slamming plates, were now dominated by a quiet, empty chair. The chair was a shrine to desperation, and each glance towards it was a remembrance of hurt. Conversations that were once fluid and effortless now floundered across unnoticed obstacles. The words became a minefield; subjects that were once considered safe are now a risk. We walked around the hole that was in our centre, and in the tense dance, a vast distance was created. Many hid behind emotional fortresses and found it more comfortable to avoid the sharp edges of their emotions.

The trust-building block on which the family's edifice was built was ripped up with a violent thud. There was still a cloud of suspicion. Every interaction from the past was scrutinised in a fresh, scathing way. Every memory was scrutinised. The trust, simple and taken for granted, that was once shared between us must now be meticulously rebuilt, brick by brick, and mortar by mortar, which was sluggish and weak.

This was the abyss of emotional ruins that a simple truth began to take into my soul, a truth I would tell Srinivas in the darkest of evenings: ***"Sometimes, the most beautiful gardens are grown not in fertile soil, but in the cracks of broken foundations."***

In the same way that our family's story seemed to be one that was a pure fracture, another story was being written that was a quiet, enduring development. The very act of living through the shared trauma started to redefine the concept of "family. It wasn't only a bloodline or shared name; it was a choice. It was a decision to stay. The choice to confront those who are ugly, humiliating, and depressing, with one another. This wasn't the family we inherited. This was a family we were building on hard-earned affection, with swollen hands and aching hearts.

As Srinivas and I worked to heal the wounds of others in our lives, we noticed our own bonds changing. Our love was not simply a romantic affair of sunny walking and sharing dreams. It was born through the ashes of this tragedy. It grew into a relationship that could feel the power of a grieving smile, which could speak the weight of a tragedy in one constant glance across a tension-filled space. It was a love that had seen the worst but was determined to look for the most positive. We were more than just friends in this life; we were allies in a battle for healing, and we formed a strong, steely bond.

As if the universe itself was giving us a way to counter our sadness, a new opportunity was presented to me. In the midst of all the confusion, the door flew open to a long-held desire. It was my turn to take on the job of Marketing Executive at an eminent product-based company. It was more than an opportunity to change jobs; it was like an opportunity to save a lifeline from afar, a sunny beach.

The decision to step into the role was a way to reclaim a part of me that the chaos in my family had obliterated. It was a place where strategy and creativity coexisted, and I was able to build and develop rather than sort through the mess of broken trust. The tasks of establishing brand differentiation and interacting with customers provided a haven for my thoughts. In the realm of data analytics and marketing strategies, I discovered my own rhythm, a goal that transcended the pain of my family.

I can remember the day I got the invitation. A burgeoning hope, a fragile optimism, was shattered through the grey emotional cloak. I ran to Srinivas, the official letter in my hand as if it were a talisman. "My love, look," I exclaimed, my voice tingling with exuberance and nervousness. "This... It's everything I've worked so hard for. It's my time to shine."

My face was taken into his hands, his fingers scrubbing away tears that I had never felt drop. In his eyes, for the first time in weeks, I saw a reflection of myself, uncoloured by sadness. "I am so proud of you," the man said, and his voice was full of emotion. "You will not only excel in this position, but you'll also set the stage with your radiance. It's your turn." The faith of his father was the breeze that blew under my wings. It was a potent reminder that, even amid a massive storm, the individual stars would still shine.

My father, too, after hearing the news, spoke words that acted as an elixir. "You have always had a light within you," the man said, his tiredness temporarily lifted by the pride of a father. "No shadow, however deep, can extinguish it. Let sparkle." In that moment, I realised that happiness for oneself is not an act of denial of the collective grief and can actually be the most potent remedy.

The brother's departure was the final straw for ignorance and the end of the family as a clean, perfect unit. However, it was also an opportunity to begin. It prompted a painful and necessary change. We discovered that honour does not mean the inability to fail, but rather the respect with which we confront it. Respectability is far more important than authenticity. Those bonds that stretch but do not crack are the ones that are worth keeping.

Srinivas, as well as I, emerged from the flames unscathed, and the fire was extinguished. We have a love story imprinted by the scars that are part of the topography as proof of its existence. The family bonds that are left may be more secluded; however, they are infinitely more authentic. They do not rely on presumption, but on a conscious decision, not based on a perfect time, but on a flawed, lasting presence.

My journey as a marketing executive grew into more than a career. It was my way of creation during a time of devastation, a testament to the truth that, although we aren't able to manage the storms that batter our home, we can choose to start a new fire, in tandem with the scattered but still glowing sparks. In the light of that fire, we can see one another and the bond that carried us through with greater clarity than ever.

GIFTS OF NEW BEGINNINGS

My story isn't made of a single thread; it's an entire tapestry. If you asked me when I first felt the shuttle move swiftly, weaving dark strands together with the gold, I'd present you with a calendar; my hand is not resting on a date, but on a specific season: the spring of 2019. A time of trembling leaves and heart-shaking trembling, all I learned about love, strength, and destiny was stripped away and re-stitched by an energy that was greater than any career goal.

It started in March, with a snore. Not a quiet one, however, but the tense metallic type that comes with an unspoken diagnosis from a doctor. My Srinivas, my anchor, who had laughed, was the soundtrack to my own personal orchestra and was suddenly lost in an ocean of uncertainty in the field of medicine. Our vocabulary was dwindling to a sombre one, including test results, doctor names, and quiet conversations in hospital hallways that smelled of antiseptics and trepidation. The bright future we had sketched out, a collage of dreams shared and secluded retirement plans, appeared to be dying of colour and washed away by dark, cold light.

I can remember sitting at his bedside at night, watching the pulsing motion of the screen cast a blue glow over his sleepy face. My personal world was, at one time, full of strategies for marketing and imaginative campaigns, but it seemed distant and unimportant. What was the relationship between click-through rates and the sacred and terrifying rate of the beat of his heart? The old skin from my previous life, which I referred to as, was not just being shed and melted by the blaze of this calamity. We were exposed, raw and two souls held to one another in the midst of a sudden roaring wind.

In that raw view, I saw an affection I'd only dreamed about. It was not the romantic love of whispered promises and sunsets. This was the love of determination. The way that my hand, shivering with its own fear and trembling, would steadily smooth his forehead. It was the silent eye contact over a plate of uncooked food from the hospital, a whole discussion of hope, fear and unwavering support flowing between us without saying a word. We were no longer friends; we were soldiers in the trenches, our love was the only weapon we had against the assault of fear.

As April slid into the month, timid and hesitant, the idea of change was no longer an abstract notion to improve one's career; it was our daily, grim life. We created a new mode of living. The kitchen became an apothecary for healing. I, the one who wrote brands, now make nutritious meals, every vegetable sliced with prayer, each smoothie mixed with a prayer for health. Easy physiotherapy sessions replaced the evenings we spent watching films and chatting. My arm's support was both physical and emotional. In the midst of fatigue, the ferocious, stoic patience it demanded, I discovered an odd, intimate connection. I was absorbing the contours of his determination by recording the peaks of his anger and the solitary peak of his resolve.

Then, a flimsy green shot of hope broke through the hard earth of April. Better test results. A day of less pain. A hint of his old smile, as if the sun was breaking through the heavy cloud cover. In this dim sunshine, a career opportunity I'd worked for years finally came to fruition, and I was offered the position of Marketing Executive at an industry-leading product-based company, beginning on the 20th of May.

The magnitude of the event was awe-inspiring. How was I able to take on a leadership role and be required to be energetic and visionary while my own life was a relic of vulnerability and vigilance? I stared at the letter, its clean paper smacking against my fingers that were still sore because I held the man with such a tight grip. My old self would've jumped without hesitation. The person I was in those hospital rooms paused as she sank to the edge of a cliff.

The person who pushed me forward was Srinivas, who gently pulled me aside. His voice, while still weaker than usual, was full of conviction. "This thread is yours," the man stated, his eyes resting on mine with the fervour of those solitary, long nights. "You must not drop it. Our tapestry would be less beautiful without it. We weave it. For you. For us."

The faith of his father was the thread that helped me start over.

The 20th of May, 2019, was not greeted with a rousing welcome and giddy excitement, but rather with calm reverence and sacred silence. I was dressed to go out for the first time at work, and the blazer's fabric felt a bit shaky after a week of soft, cozy sweaters. I gave Srinivas a goodbye kiss that smelt of shared storms as well as an uneasy, new peace. The moment I stepped into the workplace was like walking across a bridge between two realms. The air smelled of optimism and fresh coffee without iodine or anxiety. For a short time, I felt split in two: the caregiver, the anxious spouse, and the professional, the strategist.

Then a magical transformation took place. While I was sitting in my new chair, listening to the difficulties of my first project, I realised that the skills developed through the intense crucible of months of endurance, empathy, and the ability to think strategically under extreme pressure were beginning to spill over into my work. The dark desert of fear sucked up the creative spark I believed sprang from a deeper, more authentic knowing. I realised that the right strategies aren't just about avoiding risks; instead, it's about navigating them with a sense of. Proper communication isn't just about clever slogans; it's about connecting to a fundamental human need for faith, optimism, and a brighter tomorrow. I'd just spent a few months in that unfiltered human space.

Each job became more than a chore. It was a way to reclaim. The process of launching a campaign was like making a small memorial to normality, an era where joy and purpose were still possible. The excitement at work was no longer just office buzz. For me, it was a music of life that was moving forward, which was a symphony I believed I'd never again hear. When I was satisfied here, I was not letting go of my home and family, and I was recognising the love that we created. I was proving to myself and to him that we were able not just to endure, but actually to make.

And Srinivas? In his home, He weaved his personal story of recovery, with each step a triumph that we celebrated with the enthusiasm of a celebration. Our evenings weren't filled with medical records, but rather with the ecstatic recounts of my day and his enthusiastic reports on his progress. We were literally recovering together. The love that was an enclave was now an organic garden, and we were tending it together.

I came up with a catchy phrase for us in those tense months as a personal remark I would whisper to him while we slept, our hands tied: ***"Love is the quiet warp upon which the loud weft of life is woven; without its steadfast strength, the most vibrant patterns would unravel."*** He was my constant warp, strong, solid, the under-appreciated base. The triumphs, the struggles, and the workplace triumphs, and the health concerns were loud and vivid wefts. Without his constant presence, my pattern and our pattern would have long ago become a knot.

The months of March and May were the time of radical metamorphosis. We were pushed to the limits of our abilities. We learned that love is more than an attractive feeling; it's a **choice** to become our own sanctuary. Professional success isn't independent of personal loss and can even be its phoenix emerging from the ashes of fear, with wings made of hard-earned wisdom.

As I look back over the tranquil distance of time, I can see the tapestry clearly. These dark threads from March aren't something to be hidden from or resentful of. They bring the illusion of depth, contrast, and significance to the sparkling gold of the 20th of May. They make the overall picture more authentic. The struggles were indeed a ripe seed that grew into a tenacity I didn't know I had, into a passion I'd not yet fully explored, and into a professional career infused with a mission more profound than any professional award.

Our story was told one thread at a time, which is a testament to the fact that the most stunning designs often come from the strength to carry the shuttle in both darkness and light, with love leading the thread. In that process, we discovered the most unexpected and irresistible gift: a relationship that wasn't just about sharing a life but also about saving and reclaiming the experience, all in one.

A TEST OF VOWS

Life, with its endless and sometimes mischievous wisdom, does not provide us with a roadmap. It provides a compass; its needle flits between happiness and despair. The real difficulty isn't knowing the direction, but instead maintaining the steady hand in your lap during a storm. My name is only a whisper in this story, as this isn't just my story; it is ours, a story told not with grand gestures under the sun's rays; however, it is written in the calm and desperate light of a hospital monitor with the beat of a heartbeat trying to keep up with mine. The story is about Srinivas and me, and the day that our journey to get married turned into an exploration into the most intimate chambers of our affection.

The morning was chaotic and joyful. Saris of gold and emerald were arranged on fresh sherwanis, and the air was sweet from the scent of sandalwood and the excitement. We were scheduled to take the train to Nashik to witness an elopement between Srinivas's most senior friend. Srinivas, my lively, humorous husband who could soothe my most angsty thoughts, was the perfect portrait of joy. He sang old films as he packed his bags, his eyes moving around the edges with plans for a dance and celebration. I looked at him with a jolly thing, and I thought about how my life has been a series of extraordinary, everyday miracles like a shared smile at breakfast or a casual stroke of fingers when we walked through the hall, the eerie hope in the midst of a bustling room.

When the train sped out from the station, the city melted in a green blur. A slight shift happened. The ebullient symphony began to fall off. Srinivas's enthralling observation of the landscape became more tense and eventually stopped. The eyes of Srinivas, typically so bright, appeared to dim, obscured by a tiredness that seemed too intense, too abrupt. He dismissed it as a night of lost rest, yet a chilly, familiar finger of fear was tracing its way into my back. This was much more than fatigue. It was a gentle evaporation from his soul, an eerie tinge of pallor in place of his usual glow. The curve hop he'd been throwing was not a joyful bounce, but an earthquake, concealed beneath the surface of a party.

The discomfort grew worse at an alarming rate. The pain grew into intense discomfort, and then it became a sharp, stabbing pain. My solid, steady Srinivas fell apart, his face stained with pain that sucked away my breath. His skin sank to the colour of ash, his breathing was an erratic, stuttering struggle. The joyous cacophony of the train compartment - laughter, the tea cup clatter--suffocated into a distant roar. And was replaced by the loud sound of my own anxiety. "Something is wrong," I mumbled, and my words became a screaming shout in my head. At that point, the world slowed down to the void between the seats. Each second seemed like a speck of sand sliding through a fist clenched, and each one was greater in value than the one before.

However, within that fear, humanity blossomed. Strangers, fellow passengers just minutes earlier, became our angels of protection. A doctor, thankfully aboard, acted with the utmost calm. The railway staff acted with rapid efficiency. A circle of worry formed around us, creating a refuge of compassion moving with the speed of the train. When we arrived at Lonavala, the final decision was taken: the journey to happiness ended. The new and urgent trip was about to begin.

The train's unscheduled stop was a brief moment of suspended time. The usual bustle dissipated, replaced by a calm, focused pressure. Hands flung out to help, and voices offered reassuring assurances. We were escorted off, not onto a sun-splashed platform full of holiday-makers, but into the arms of an ambulance waiting to be rolled into the scene, its siren wailing in stark, wailing praise to the new reality we live in. The journey to the hospital in town consisted of swaying streets, my hands firmly his, muttering not the romantic songs from the past but rather frantic, prayerful prayers that were rooted in the foundations: "Stay. Please, stay."

"In the anatomy of a crisis, you do not find your character; you meet it, raw and unfamiliar, in the mirror of your beloved's fear."

The following 15 days at Nashik Hospital were a lifetime in the white walls. Life splintered into an unending and uneasy equilibrium with the uninspiring vigil that was held at his bedside, with the only music being the hum from the ECG and the sluggish rhythm of his breath. The quiet calls in the corridors, where I fought to keep a professional life that was now an unreal, distant place. My profession, which had been, for a time, a significant part of my self-identity, became an echo of it. The only essential thing was the man lying in the bed, fighting for a cause whose nuances we had only begun to comprehend.

While he sat there with his hand limp, I learned about the actual discussion of prioritisation. It wasn't an intellectual process, but rather the sensation of tearing. Everything--ambitions, social obligations, even the basic mechanics of eating and sleeping--fell away until only the bedrock remained: love. The vows we'd previously made under a floral-adorned mandap "in sickness and in health" changed from a poetic vow into a more practical, daily liturgy. I washed his face and coaxed him to drink water, and became the interpreter for his pain to the nurses, and became his anchor within the swirling, meditative confusion.

The diagnosis, once it arrived, was a physical strike. It explained the attack on the body, but it also brought another blow to our spirits. In the darkest of his moments, in which fear and pain caused him to look away from the eyes of his, I witnessed not only my husband's vulnerability but also my own vulnerability reflected. It wasn't his experience, and he was not the only one to suffer. It was ours. Our strength was no longer a single thing; it was woven into a fabric. My strength was an option that he could use after his reserves were exhausted, and his stoic determination to fight kept my faith burning. We were two trees caught in an avalanche, and our roots were tangled deep beneath the ground that the fierce wind could not uproot one with the help of another.

The outside world continued to spin in an uneventful course. The emails piled up, deadlines disappeared, and I had to make the only decision that made sense: I quit my job. In a culture that often mistakenly prioritises work, I was able to express my peaceful protest. It was a statement that, in the heart's hierarchy, love is the most important calling. It was not a sacrifice but rather a claim. I wasn't shedding the title, but was completely embracing my most important job: being his partner and advocate. I was the one who carried our common light.

And we weren't the only ones. The echoes of other love stories surrounded us. Families and friends weaved an enveloping net under us. They came not with apologies, however, but with practicality. home-cooked food that smelled of love, peaceful company that didn't require an avalanche of messages that stated, "We are here." They served as reminders that our personal struggle was being watched, that our love was part of the larger community of compassion.

After an extremely exhausting day, a fantastic thing happened. It was like the lines on Srinivas's skin finally loosened. The hard breath slowed into the gentle, even flow. He fell asleep, a tranquil, peaceful sleep. I watched the rise and fall of his chest in the dim light and the bright orange glow of a streetlight, drawing his silhouette in soft relief. In that quiet, sacred space the anxiety that was an ever-present tightness in my abdomen started in the beginning, to ease. The struggle was not over; however, the tide was shifting.

The time of recovery in the gentle, slow months that followed, his gratitude surfaced   not as a formal expression, but as a powerful force. We discovered the joy of celebration in the smallest of victories: the first sentence which he could not resist, the first tentative walk along the hospital's corridor, and his hands in mine. We came to appreciate a deep admiration for the silent moments of simple delights, like the warm morning sun warming his face through the windows, and the quiet, shared laughter over absurd food in a hospital, at a dinner that was solely about peace and tranquillity, without the burden of the moment to come.

A few days later, while I read to him, he reached out and took my hand. His voice, though weak, was a reflection of all the weight that the world has. "Your presence," he stated, his eyes gripping mine with a fervour that transcended his physical fragility, "has been my anchor. In the deepest of seas, I felt your anchor holding me tight towards this world, in your hands." One tear fell, tracing a track down his cheek. It was a tear that showed no weaknesses, but only the utter and vulnerable power of a love that has been tested and proved. Through the tear, I could see the whole journey of our relationship reflected: the terror, the struggle and the unflinching grasp.

Our journey didn't lead us to the wedding ceremony. It took us to something more profound and to the core of our love. The train ride that started with laughter didn't end in defeat, but in an intense dive into what it means to be loved. We realised that love isn't only the spark that enflames the flame for a lifetime, but also the constant, unstoppable flame that burns throughout the long, cold winter nights. It's the determination to make an anchor and the strength to hang on to it.

When I see Srinivas returning to health and happiness, I learn more about the man I married. I can see the struggle we won, the quiet-spoken language of love we have now learned, as well as the growing depth of understanding in his eyes. The story we tell is testimony not to a love that withstood this storm but to one who learned to dance, unwavering and confident, even through torrential rain. It's proof that the most breathtaking places are usually the ones that we had no intention of reaching, and that the most enduring bonds are formed not through comfort and comfort, however, but through the sacred flame of the crucible of shared perseverance. This is where we are destined to end up. And I'd take this route, along with him, many times over.

THE HEART OF SACRIFICE

"They claim that love is a beautiful feeling reserved for romantic sunsets and whispered promises. I've discovered that the truest expression of love can be located somewhere else. It's in the clean smell of a hospital's area, the exact amount of medication taken at 2 am and in the peaceful, solid grasp of a hand that does not allow you to sink into the murky waters. It is not only my story. It's the life story of a heart. Not the one that was unable to beat and failed, but the multitude of hearts that discovered, despite all odds, to defeat the more powerful."

December 18, 2019. The date was not etched in ink, but rather in the bitter, metallic taste of terror. The evening began with the normal symphony that played in our home, the clattering of dishes, the hum of a heater, and the distant roar of a TV show. Then, the phone rang. One breathless sentence from my mother-in-law, and the familiar patterns of our lives were broken into the most tense, breathless fragments.

My father-in-law, who was a man of large laughter and hands that could repair any issue, was struck by a solitary inner lightning bolt, a heart attack.

The next few minutes are images painted in the harsh, bright hues of anxiety, the rush of panicked people to their house. The sight of him, grey and writhing across the ground, was a symbol of strength that was suddenly incredibly fragile. The scream of our past lives replaced the ambulance's siren. At the rear of this car, my mother-in-law's screams as the percussion, and the paramedic's sharp words as the music, I held his icy hand. I was thinking, at times, in a bizarre way, about his watch. It was still going on. *What was it that could cause it to continue to tick?*

The hospital's waiting area was a place of shared fear. Strangers were huddled in islands filled with anxiety, breathing the same antiseptic-scented air of despair and hope. Time, once a reliable river, was now an ooze. Minutes grew into arid periods of time. It was in this vast void that I found my anchor.

Srinivas…

He didn't come into the room; he simply stood *present*. An unstoppable, warm touch on my shoulder. He spoke only a few words, yet his voice was one I could understand. In the chaos, his quiet was a whispered sonnet. He took a cup of terrible coffee, spoke to the doctors in a soft, steady voice, and his eyes, as they met mine, were the world of our shared understanding. We weren't just spouses at that point. We were also travellers who were tossed off to the same dangerous sea. The only thing that could guide us was our devotion to the man who was fighting behind those swinging doors.

> ***"Crisis is not a way to make a person, but it does reveal them. In the ruins of a typical day, I spotted the outline of my husband's soul, and it was made from a sluggish, indestructible steel."***

As we finally got to view our loved one in the ICU, the sight sucked my breath. There, in a maze of wires and blinking devices, there was the father of our family, diminished to a flimsy body in a bleached dress. He appeared less imposing. The only indications that he was alive were the pulsating, hypnotic sound of the monitor for cardiac health and the slow rising and falling in his chest. The beep *sound of... sound... and beep* was to become the new heartbeat for our family. A digital metronome is a device that tracks the unpredictable rhythm of our survival.

The recovery of his father was a delicate bridge that we had to construct each day with a gruelling effort. As the oldest daughter-in-law, the responsibilities of primary caregiver fell on my shoulders, not through ceremonies, but rather as a gentle, unavoidable burden. It was a position I took not solely out of obligation but out of a source of love I'd never believed I had.

Our house was transformed. The living room was transformed into an inpatient unit, and the kitchen became a dietary pharmacy. My day started before dawn and was choreographed to the demands of a recovering heart. I was a researcher of beta-blockers and sodium counts and a master of pill organisers, which jangled like savage maracas. I was able to discern the obscure language of medical records and take a bath with a gentle man who once lifted me onto his shoulders to act as a steady arm for slow, strenuous strolls to the garden.

It was a new reality for me: I was performing a delicate dance that was exhausting. I danced between mixing the soup with low cholesterol, helping my kids with their homework, scheduling echocardiograms, and paying household bills. My personal demands were neatly folded and then disappeared into the dusty corners of my head. There was no space for them. My world was confined to the walls surrounding our house and the vital indicators of one man.

In the confines of this world, I encountered unexpected moments of grace. The first time, he could manage to speak a complete word without going into a gasp. The genuine, but weak smile he gave after consuming an oat I'd laboured over. The way his eyes, swollen with trauma and medications, might clear and reveal mine, expressing the most profound gratitude, caused me to cry quietly on my own. While tending to his physical skeleton, I gained access to the vulnerable, gentle side of him. This was an esoteric relationship.

The truth is that no love story has no adversaries, and we often feature the face of worried love. My mother-in-law, who was engulfed by her own puddle of fear and despair, was an integral part of my care. Her devotion to the man she loved was a ferocious, passionate flame that possessed her, and in her rage, she sometimes smouldered those who tried to aid her.

Her eyes were always under inspection. A pinch less salt, a blanket that was adjusted five minutes late, or a pill containing water instead of juice could be a sign of failure. "That's not how he likes it," she would tell me in her voice, her voice as if trying to find a seam. "Are you sure the doctor said that?" The anxiety manifested as snarky, and her scrutiny felt like a rebuke during my most exhausting days.

There were times when I would go to the laundry room. It was the one space where the machine's sound would make my sobs sound less silent. The scent of fabric softener was mingled with my tears' salt. Did I do enough? Am I doing enough? Her words, which are often not meant to cause pain in the heart, left a mark on my already swollen spirit.

"The heaviest weights are not the ones you lift for others, but the invisible stones of disapproval placed upon your spirit by those you're trying to help."

It was in this place of doubtful dedication that I learned a painful, beautiful lesson. Actual sustained caregiving cannot be an act of applause or performance. It must be an act of hidden integrity and not performed to the crowd inside the venue, but instead for the silent audience of my conscience. I was able to hear her critique, and to view it not as an expression from my heart, but as the deformed echo of her own anxiety. My love for my father-in-law was to be an inner, resilient power, unaffected by the validation. It was dressed in an apron, used a calculator to measure milligrams, then bit its tongue. It was a love which did its work in silence.

Through it all, there was Srinivas. If this time was one of war, it was not only my fellow soldier, but he was also my haven in the shadows. Our relationship, which was once built with leisurely meals and planned getaways, was rekindled during the peaceful late hours of the night, watching.

He was the one who kept my shards. In the evenings, when I emerged from the ward and my shoulders sank with a weight that was not visible, he would accompany me to the kitchen, pour me an iced tea, and then just listen. He didn't give me unsubstantiated advice or quick solutions. He provided the profound benefit of seeing exhaustion. His still strength was the foundation that my frayed endurance could grow.

I can recall a particular night. It was well past midnight, and the house was in the deep, suffocating silence of despair. Doubts, like sneaky vines, were engulfing my head. I thought: You're not doing enough. This isn't possible. The family is crumbling. Children are being neglected. I am sitting at the table with my head in my hands, empty.

Then I felt his hands over my shoulders. Warm, solid. He didn't speak. He began to work the tension of my rock-hard muscles; his hand was more profound than words. It was saying, "I am here. It said, "You're not alone." We are all burdened by this. Then he moved a chair closer, took my hand, and placed it on his heart. I could feel its steady rhythm under my fingers.

"This is my rhythm," he said, his voice shaky from emotions and sleep. "And the beat is for you. The beat is *together with* you. No matter how chaotic it is out there, here we're in the same place. We'll navigate this, Meera. Don't just get through it. Take it on. Together."

The time was much more personal than any kiss and more romantic than any gesture of grandeur. It was the union of souls in darkness. Our love wasn't an individual, joyful entity; it was the foundational wall that prevented the whole, fragile framework of our life from crashing.

Months of blood poured into a year. The acute illness was tempered into a more prudent normal. My father-in-law's health slowly and miraculously improved. The alarm was replaced by the constant, comforting laughter of his return, with a softer tone yet real. The edge that was critical to my mother-in-law's voice slowly dwindled and was sometimes replaced with an uneasy, and at times, grateful, gratitude.

I came out of this long, chilly season not the same person as I was when I had entered it. I was a mess. I was prone to circles around my eyes that reflected the countless moments of vigilance, as well as a newfound resilience in my spine. The relationship I had with Srinivas was tense and on the verge of breaking. We'd seen each other in a raw state, stretched to the limit, then decided each day to bend in front of each other and not fall apart.

We discovered our love story in a moment of snooze, a glance at his father's eyes when he reminisced about an old tale and a toast in silence with our eyes following the appointment of a good doctor and the way that our fingers would search our partner's gaze in the secluded darkness of our bedroom and a bond that was pure, unspoken understanding.

The story of my life is not a tragedy. It's a love story. It is a romantic love story of the inside one that does not make for cinema with a grand scale, and instead, it is a story of a highly loving life.

It's the story of love for a man that taught me the importance of fragility. Family love that stretched and stretched, but eventually was held. A passionate, private self-love that I discovered through my unwavering self-confidence. Above all, it can be described as a marriage love that was stripped of its glamour and found, underneath, not to be mere passion or friendship, but a deep, active *loyalty*.

"They refer to heartbeats as a part of romantic love. We came to a deeper understanding. Our love wasn't a single heartbeat, but rather the entire system of circulation, the vein which carried the load and the artery that provided the force, and the continuous rhythm between two people which kept the entire beautiful, wounded organism of 'us'."

It was a cold, dark December night. The heart was attacked. In response, many of my heart, Srinivas's, and our family's hearts fought and reacted with ferocity. The love we had never realised that we had. We did more than survive. We loved. In the constant, gentle act of love, we discovered the most romantic of all: that written in the ink of everyday life, in sacrifice, and signed by a tired, but happy, caregiver.

THE FREELANCE ODYSSEY

If I make it all the way through the book's pages, its spine would wear soft by rereading the book, and its margins would be stained by salt from tears of despair as well as the water of the Goan Sea. This isn't just an academic journal; it's the heart's map, as well as a personal account written with the two inks of devotion and struggle. It is the tale of how I navigated a path through professional uncertainty, guided by two stars: my inner strength and a bond that served as my anchor. The story begins with a truth imprinted in my heart: ***"Triumph is an ongoing journey; defeat does not define you."*** This was my daily mantra, and the very first line of my tale.

My life as a freelancer began in solitude, a canvas stretched out with ambition and trepidation. The path wasn't that straight sunlit route I imagined, but rather a winding trail of shadows and surprising illumination. There were times when self-doubt, the long-standing and sly enemy, would surround my dreams and tighten its grip until I couldn't breathe. I would look at a blank screen, with the silence roaring louder than any critique. Was I foolish to believe that I could create a new world entirely from nothing other than my own mind?

However, I could hear my mentor's voice in my memory, an ethereal yet firm sound. Mentor's Name taught me to look at things using different eyes. "Look at the setback," they would advise, "not as a wall, but as a door you haven't found the handle to yet." Their knowledge helped me to see my stumbles differently. Each pitch that was rejected, each quiet client, every project that was frayed at the edges. These weren't flamboyant words of rejection; they were dark, rich soil. These were occasions to shed confidence and water patience in anticipation of the more robust and more stunning sprouts of strength to burst through.

The ability to endure, I discovered, is not a screaming fire. It is the steady, steadfast flame of a pilot lamp which never dims. It was my most powerful allies, the quietest. I worked hard, one word, one style, or one page of code at a time. With each completed project, each note of customer satisfaction, I didn't feel the roar of triumph; instead, a deep, high-pitched confirmation of the core truth. The success I experienced was not just the distant city that was situated on the top of a hill, but the ground that I was attempting to stand on, a bit unsteady and real beneath my feet.

However, no artist creates work in the absence of. I quickly realised that my single canvas was part of a vast, interconnected gallery. Networking, a term that's often secluded from its meaning in business guides, was revealed to me as one of the most human art forms. It wasn't the card exchange that was cold or the casual meeting of minds. The spark was an idea over a cup of coffee. The warm introduction, the surprise "I have a friend who ..."

The lesson of connectivity found its most authentic expression at MH Technosoft. I entered through a gate that was opened by the kinship of my brother-in-law's friend. It was an easy moment of connection that turned into a vital lifeline. As a Content Analyst, I began my career with all my academic rigour and a fervent dedication to the job. However, I'm convinced that destiny prefers those who are connected. Serendipity was woven into those threads that make up these connections, creating a Zilli Funny Videos project. In a flash, I wasn't just an analyst, but a conductor, given the baton that would lead an orchestra I'd not yet met.

The creation of that team was an act of creative love. I travelled not just across India but also across the landscape of dreams that sought not only technicians and storytellers but also employees and people who believed in it. In bustling cafes and quiet homes, I met people whose eyes lit up with the same amazing, mad vision. We were a web of diverse threads, diverse backgrounds, accents and talents, all united through a common conviction in the power of storytelling and laughter. "A business is an orchestra," I'd say to them. "Your unique note is essential. Use it with confidence." We formed an alliance in which rivalry dissolved into respect, and collective power made us a success.

In all the solo struggles and collective triumphs, there was a steady, regular rhythm: Srinivas. He was the calm harbour for my tense ship. I was the unwavering defender of my faith when my personal belief waned. Our love story was different from my professional journey. It was the soothing background music that added dimension and meaning.

This draws my attention to Goa. In the evening, the sky put on a nightly wonder show, a blaze of orange and a blush of pink. In the evening, the Arabian Sea whispered secrets to the shore. There in the sand that was still warm between our toes, I knew everything. In tandem with Srinivas, I was more than just a freelancer; I was an executive leader striving. I was simply an individual whom everyone loved. This was more than Valentine's Day; it was an act of thanksgiving. Thanks for the journey, for each deviation that brought me to this point and also for the person who was there with me every step of the way.

The gentle waves traced patterns of lace around our feet. I glanced at the back. I saw the nervous novice, the team-builder with determination, and the tenacious freelancer. I observed the late evenings and early mornings, the wins toasted with chai, and his calming silence softened the losses. This arduous, uncertain adventure not only shaped the foundation of a successful career but also laid the foundation of our friendship. It showed us that love isn't just about celebrating the summit and rejoicing over every step together.

My canvas of today is no longer solely mine. It's filled with the vibrant colours of collaboration, textured with the hard-earned lessons, and illuminated by the golden light of a shared existence. The path to freelancing is full of unexpected turns, but I approach it with different eyes. I consider each project a chapter waiting to be written. I see each connection as a novel character in my tale.

At the end of each day, I return to my core and my love. To the realisation that the most significant triumph isn't a title or an account balance, but a life lived with intention and a firm heart. My journey continues with a constant personal love letter to my art, which shapes my life, to the strength that keeps me going, and to my husband, Srinivas, whose love is the peaceful, beautiful destination at every step.

"Life, like the ocean, doesn't require that we master it, but that we embark with a strong heart and an arm to support us at dusk, that is gathering. The greatest victory can be not found in the tranquil harbour and the calm sea, instead, in stories that we tell in the wild, beautiful, wild, and uncontrolled journey."

FINDING STRENGTH IN CHANGE

My story isn't one of the fairy tales that begin in "once upon a time." Instead, it is a tale of enduring the storms that I faced on my own, and then, in a miraculous way, with others. It's a memoir of a heart's learning to beat with another. It is set against the backdrop of my life created with my own two, sometimes trembling hands. If I had to identify the moment when the story's narrative changed forever, the point where the protagonist realised the solitary battle was ended, and that was February 14, 2020, on the beach in Goa. This was the day that my life, in its most authentic and most vivid sense, started.

Before Srinivas, there was a sea of freelancers. An immense, thrilling, and terrifying sea of my own work that I decided to explore. My vessel was constructed from the strength of my will and a stack of credit cards that were maxed out, and my compass was a flimsy conviction of my voice. There were years of food and years of feasting, moments of exhilarating victory, but matched by the hollow and gnawing fear of an inbox that was empty. I was taught that resilience was not a buzzword, but rather a bone-deep survival strategy. I came to myself in the dark early hours of the morning, a person terrified but determined. The journey, despite its arduous sacrifices, made me into someone I could admire. It taught me that I could remain on my own. However, it did not show me how I needed to.

Enter Srinivas. He came not as a rescue vessel, however, but rather as an oath-taking fellow seaman who saw the face of one who charted uncharted waters. Our relationship was not a flashy storm, but an ebb and flow rising tide that was steady and patient, slowly claiming each dry shore of my solitude. On the second Valentine's Day, we were an entity, a partnership, but Goa... Goa was to be our destination.

We picked Goa not because of its popularity as a party destination; we chose it for its deep feelings, for its ancient palms that whispered mysteries towards the Arabian Sea, for its beaches that were home to an inscription of thousands of tales. It was a place that felt eternal and instant, just as the love I discovered. The evening, we walked together, the world became a symphony of the senses. The sandy beach, which remained warm after the day's sunshine, had a silky, gold-coloured texture under our feet. The air was perfumed with frangipani and salt and distant spices, a smell of freedom. The sea, the eternal, breathing thing, painted itself in shades of sapphire and turquoise. The rhythmic crashing and sigh were the only sound we needed.

As the sun began to set, the skies put on a fantastic show for us. It changed from a fiery, intense orange to an ethereal, optimistic pink. The colours were so fierce that they appeared to saturate not only the sky but my soul. With that glowing glow, Srinivas stopped. He turned his attention to me, and the sun's setting rays illuminated his eyes with an intense light that had nothing to do with the sky. The world sat in its breath. The waves stopped in their chant.

"You," he said in a soft, vibrating voice that I felt deep in my soul, "you never cease to amaze me."

They were easy to understand. However, they weren't simple in the sense of being easy. They held in them the late nights he'd stayed up to watch me work, every annoyance I'd sucked through his shoulders, and every tiny victory he'd gushed about as if it was his own. His appreciation was like an encasement, wrapping the anxious, cold parts of my freelance experience and transforming them into something more beautiful. It was a reaffirmation of my personal journey, sure, but, more importantly, it was a pious acknowledgement of *his love for us and our* journey. It was a love that didn't simply watch from shore, but went out into the dark, uncertain water with me.

"A life built alone teaches you strength, but a love built together teaches you the purpose for which that strength was meant." That's the quote that I will inscribe into my personal history. I was able to comprehend it at the moment, in that molten light of sunset.

We sat on the sand while twilight became a velvet cloak that was pinpricked by a million sparkling stars. The sky above was no longer a sky; it was a cathedral. Srinivas brought out a bottle of wine. The gentle *sound* from the cork marked the end of our silence. He poured the wine, the liquid shining in the evening light, and the glass was raised. His eyes were fixed as a promise was made.

"To new beginnings," the man said, his voice filled with emotion. "And for us. We are stronger together."

The crystal sang when our glasses collided, with a crystal-clear, bright note in the humid air, which I associate with destiny. "To us," I repeated, my words swollen with a deep gratitude that tasted like tears. It was more than an intimate toast. This was a contract. A silent pledge made on the edge of a wine glass, and witnessed by the universe itself, to ensure that our different paths would become irrevocably joined to a common future, we would create one brick at a time and day by day.

In the calm that followed, enveloped by the symphony of waves and the sky above, I pondered. I was awestruck by the intricate web of chance and a shrewd decision that had brought me here from the solitude and stress of my workplace to the moment that I was in complete peace and harmony. The obstacles weren't gone completely, but they had been transformed. They weren't monsters anymore in my bed; they were merely mountains that we were now able to climb together, with his hands in mine, our breaths in the same cold air.

The night that I stayed at Goa was the pivot of my life's work. It concluded the first volume, which was titled "The Solitary Builder," an account of the struggle for survival and self-creation. Then, with dawn, it began the second volume, "The Architects of Us." It was a story of love not only of hearts, but also of lives. The merging of blueprints, connecting the resources of spirit, of imagining, using the singular first person.

We stayed until the last light dissipated, discussing everything and absolutely nothing of the many freelance projects to come, with his steady commitment. Of the dream home we wanted to create, not only an apartment and a house, but a place of refuge. Of the simple, deep desire to age with this tempo in our ear, the beat of our hearts and the sound of a common sea.

While I type this in the context of a study we created together, the memories of the Goa evening serve as my anchor. Life, in its beautiful, complex, messy, and dazzling beauty, is continuing to unravel. There are still challenges or professional apprehensions, days when the sea of worry gushes in. But I'm no longer facing them alone on a beach. I turn around, and there is my co-architect, my fellow sailor of my vivacious, breathing promise on a starlit beach.

February 14, 2020, was more than just a day. The day that I became more than a victim of my own experience and began to celebrate our everyday life. This was when hope was no longer a fragile, distant object and transformed into the firm, warm touch of his hand in mine. This was when the universe, in its endless imagination, drew its most gorgeous line across the sky for us. And we two lonely souls eventually learned to see and understand it all as one. The story of our lives is being written in the peaceful mornings and everyday struggles. Still, its prose will be forever written in the golden sand of Goa and the salt-scented air and in the enduring romantic echo of toasts under the stars in a blanket.

TRIALS OF THE HEART

Before you begin, remember that this isn't simply a tale of a pandemic, an accident or an illness. It's a map of a heart that is sketched by the shaking hand of healing. It's about the relationship between two people that is most true, and about how love can turn into a deliberate, brave act of wrapping up, of driving through the night, and of telling "it's okay" into the deep darkness. If you've ever been in love or broken or found a way back to yourself by the love of another or more, these pages are perfect for you.

COVID-19 was not just a way to bring the world to a halt. It also imposed a profound silence, echoing over the everyday symphony. The bustling streets that lined my windows, which were once a bustling river of humming cars and chatting pedestrians, remained as the scene of a painting. The pulsing human hum, the soundtrack of our everyday lives, dissolved into a sombre silence. For my spouse, Srinivas, and me, the four walls of our house began to look less like a place of refuge and more like a soft enclosure. The monotony was a steady and dripping tap on our souls. We wanted something new, an interruption in the routine and a sigh of unscripted air, a smack of the freedom we'd been so naively assumed to be.

When I write this, I physically relive the longing. It was an emotional hunger. So, we gave it food.

On the 1st of June 2020, we reached an agreement with the rebels. Our vehicle of escape? His trusty bike. Our aim? to feel the breeze gently touch our faces once again in search of a sense of order, not on the planet, but within the movement of the roads. It was daring, necessary, small acts of rebellion against the global chaos.

I remember clinging to him as we drove away at midnight, hearing the engine's roar an enthralling counterpoint to the quiet of the neighbourhood. The familiar streets disappeared, and we headed for the city's arteries that were asleep and then into the roads that promised to be embraced by the beauty of the natural world. The wind wasn't just an air breeze; it was an initiation. It swept away the monotony of being alone. The joy we felt, sucked up by the speed and released into the night air, was the first genuine, unadulterated joy we've felt in months. It was thrilling. At that point, I thought: *"This is us, reclaiming our narrative from the clutches of fear."*

However, the universe, as it turns out, has a method to edit our stories.

The first drop came as a shock. The second was an alert. Then, the heavens exploded furiously. It was as if a silent pandemic had been stored away, then shattered over us in a million pieces of liquid. The world was dissolved into a loud, transparent fog. The rain that fell on our helmets was a raucous drumroll, akin to bullets of water exploding at our shaky sense of adventure.

Then, it skidded. Then, a devastating low-speed loss in gravity. The time didn't stop. It broke. I could feel the bike, this vessel of freedom, change into an independent, wild thing underneath us. Then, the impact. A scorching, white-hot symphony of pain, as tough asphalt came to greet us. The relaxing adventure didn't end with a grunt, however, but with a sharp and wet crunch.

In the following moments of lying still and still in the pounding rain, the world reduced to two feelings: the cold dagger-points of the rain that soaked my body and the warm swell of blood. My head turned in, and I felt a sigh of pain and looked up to see

Srinivas standing motionless alongside me. The moment I was in that surreal, tense instant, I was struck by a powerful fact that was etched into my mind: *"Joy and chaos are not opposites, but intimate neighbours, separated by the thinnest of walls."*

The hospital was filled with glowing sterile lights and beeping machines. My face, as I first saw it on a reflective surface, appeared to be a gross mockery of itself, swollen and bruised, a scene of trauma. Every blemish was grim evidence of the brutality of the fall. The physical wounds, however severe, are only the most visible.

The real battle took place in the recovery room's silence. The fear was present in Srinivas's eyes as I looked at him, not in pity but with a desperate affection. It was the guilt I felt over my vulnerability, the fear that the image I had seen in the reflection was the person I had been. Every glance was an act of bravery and a battle with the fragility and disfigurement.

In this open space, our bond and love were questioned and tested by fire.

Srinivas never left. He was my anchor. If doubts were threatening my eyes and my mind, he would sway, and his voice would be an ethereal, steady light in the midst of pain. "It's okay," he would say. "We are okay." This simple statement became our motto. It didn't completely erase the hurt, but it created an edifice on which we could both flounder.

We started to heal together. He changed my bandages in an affectionate manner, which made me cry more than the sting of an antiseptic. We walked through the maze of frustration and fear together, and our bonds grew tighter with each shared silence and each sly smile. Our accident stripped us naked; however, through that strippedness, we felt an even deeper bond. "Love," I wrote in my journal, a bandaged hand moving slowly, "is not just seeing the beauty of the eyes of someone. It's about becoming the caretaker for their bits of brokenness and believing with all your heart in the new mosaic that will be created."

As our physical scars began to show the fate, it appeared that the lessons weren't done. The scourge remained in a continuous, low-grade fever that hung in the backdrop of our daily lives. In an attempt to find a bit of normalcy, we ordered takeout from a local favourite restaurant one night.

For a couple of golden hours, it was working. It was a return to laughter, but lighter and dancing in our tiny living room. The food was delicious, a memory of a happy past. After a while, the echo morphed into a roar inside my body. A numbing twinge grew into a gut-wrenching, excruciating pain severe food poisoning. In a society that is terrified of a single virus, my body has been a prisoner of an entirely different and intimate brutality.

The doctors in Nashik, whose faces were etched with the exhaustion caused by the pandemic, recommended that I visit specialists to treat my injuries on the face. The next step was an arduous journey through a secluded world, my body already a symbol of rebellion. However, Srinivas simply stated, "We'll go."

This journey was a different type of test. There was no night journey to freedom it was a slow determined journey through anxiety and hope. Every bump brought a jolt to my body, but as I sat next to him with my hands wrapped around his waist and my helmeted head resting upon his back, I felt a steadfast security. We weren't just going to a town; we were aiming for healing and resolving to be united. The road was not easy, but our destination was unambiguous.

Today, as I sit at my desk, I can see that the physical marks have mellowed into silvery whispers on my skin. They're no longer wounds; they are inscribed. They tell the tale of a night ride and a storm, or an accident and a long ride back. They describe resilience not as a great and heroic virtue, but as a simple daily decision to look in the mirror, return to the bike, take a bite of food, and be a lover despite the fear.

The pandemic showed us that connectivity isn't automatic; it's an option. It brought a digital chill across the globe, replacing warm smiles with pixelated smiley faces. In our own space of recovery and trauma, Srinivas and I learned that we were not the only ones. We discovered that real bonding is deeply, achingly physical. It's a hand held by pain, a soothing cloth wiped over a sweaty brow and the constant presence in a hospital bed. It's there constantly, performing the painful, uncomfortable daily task of healing.

This is not the story of a fairytale romance unharmed by the dark. It's a love-biography composed in the style of strength. It's about recognising that in the vulnerability of our most vulnerable is the greatest strength. In addition, the most lasting romance is not always found in extravagant gestures, but rather in a silent, comforting whisper in the darkness: "It's okay. I'm here. We're fine."

The stars of that night will forever be etched into my heart first as a canopy of liberty, followed by a tower that was a mess, then lastly as a testament to our unbreakable bond. We came out not harmed; however, we were transformed. The pandemic was a threat to the entire world; however, in our small world, which was two in size, it brought our love into its purest, most fundamental form: a sanctuary, a promise to each other, and an unbreakable pact against the ravages.

As such, I'm leaving you with the most authentic quote I have ever written:

"We didn't fall that night, soaked by the rain, but we were rooted. In the broken ground of our fears and bodies, we grew closer, stronger, and more firmly grounded than we would have ever been."

NAVIGATING THE STORM

The year 2020 began not in a whisper but instead with a sigh of global awe. The air seemed swollen with uncertainty, and the usual routines of life came to an abrupt halt. For me, it was a swansong occasion only in the way an event can be, A terrifying, beautiful force that sloughs everything away, leaving only the vital, underlying foundations of your life exposed. It was a time of crucible, an era of profound emotional and personal alchemy, when everything I was familiar with was destroyed in the midst of a crisis, only to be rebuilt with the strength I had never believed I had.

My job, at first an organized path, turned into an adventure through the fog. I was the leader of a team comprising between 20 and 30 beautiful, incredible, brilliant, and fearful people. Our office, a mosaic of shared meals and mumbled collaborations, disappeared overnight, replaced by the quiet of grids on video. The issue was not just operational; it was also spiritual. How do you keep a group's spirit together when the world is tearing everyone apart? The lines between personal and professional are eroding. In one frame, I could see a colleague's expression; in the other, on their monitor, a kid's toy or anxious eyes. We weren't only employees, we were people, holding on to our keyboards like lifelines.

The dynamics created an unsteady ecosystem. Each participant brought a universe of strength and struggle into our virtual world. It was a feeling of the weight, and I felt a physical strain upon my soul. My most sacred obligation was to pay attention not only to the words spoken, but also to the slow moments, the hesitations or the silence of the voice of a tired one. I often ended the day by putting my head buried in my hands and the sound of my home echoing through my ears, and I would wonder whether I had done enough. The phrase that became my motto and was written on an old Post-it near my monitor was a straightforward, sincere plea: ***"To lead is to love the chaos, and to find the music in the mismatched hearts of your tribe."***

Then, the disputes erupted at a blazing pace, personal ones that were amplified by the pressure cooker we were all in. A minor financial squabble that was once settled over coffee escalated into a raging battle of accusations among friends. The test took a toll on the bones. My hands were shaking during a mediation session, not because of fear, but because of deep sadness that pressure could be breaking bonds. I approached the issue with a surgeon's concern and a poet's compassion. We spoke not only of numbers but also of fear and security, and of the fundamental need to be fair in an uneven place. The focus was not on winning, but rather on healing. In that uncomfortable space, we came to a deeper understanding. We realized that conflict, when handled with respect, can become the most fertile soil for confidence.

My job began to change. From being a task manager, I became a potential gardener. I noticed leadership sparks in the quiet analyst in patient care, as well as in the nimble developer who worked from a shabby bedroom desk. I learned how to delegate not only tasks but also the authority. I came to believe and trust their abilities. As a result of the trust I had built, I saw a fantastic bloom. Confidences among us blossomed like wildflowers in cracks in concrete, and our collective output was transformed into a symphony by instruments that we tuned in the darkness.

However, as I tended to my colleagues, the work environment was experiencing an incredible transformation. The threat of automation loomed with a dual sword of threat and opportunity. The landscape of employment I had known was fading away, and its replacement lay in a vast, unexplored digital steppe. This is where I found an unanticipated partner, who was analysing content. In the endless stream of information and news, I began to discover patterns. The result was that it became, in a sense, a literary endeavour, studying the world's chaotic subtext. This ability became my lighthouse. **"Clarity,"** I wrote in my journal **", is not a condition one finds, but a melody one pieces together from the discordant notes of reality."** This analytical eye did not strip the world of emotion but instead gave my feelings a path to follow.

In the midst of this turmoil, A quiet, persistent idea was forming in me. It was less an idea for a business than a romantic romance that had a chance. The pandemic's isolation, even in its utter loneliness, provided me with the solitude required to listen to my heart's desire. I observed businesses drowning in information, yet hungry for clarity. I recognized the urgent necessity for an illuminating beacon to provide clarity.

So, **Cominfo Source** was conceived. It was more than just a business; it was a heartfelt love letter to the world in turmoil. It was hope, encapsulated. It was determination that was made real. The decision to walk away from the safety of my job into the unknown of business was the most terrifying and romantic decision I made in my career. It was more than just the beginning of an enterprise; I was creating an island in the storm, initially for myself and later for others.

The beginning was a tapestry that was woven with threads of pure determination and damaged nerves. My savings, and the money I had set aside for "security," were poured into this dream. Every penny was a seed that was planted with the intention of praying. The first challenges were endless; getting that first venture off the ground felt like capturing the glare of a star, and establishing our service offerings was a continuous process of creating and recreating. Financial constraints were a constant, bleak partner. There were times when the spreadsheets' numbers looked red, and the anxiety was like a shivering rock in my stomach. I would lie awake, the burden of my team's financial security and the future of my family weighing on me like a physical anchor in my chest.

In that battle, I discovered a fierce passion for the task. Every failure became a knowledge, a puzzle which, when completed, strengthened us. We adopted a philosophy of fluid adaptation and gained knowledge from every failure and win. Data-driven decisions were our compass; however, the intuition we forged during the nights of sleep was our northern star.

To help my brand-new, small, bold team, I created virtual workshops. These were not boring instruction sessions. These were gatherings of the heart. We shared screens and talked about our fears. We mastered Python and worked on empathy. I observed that as technical abilities and emotional intelligence developed, this virtual space became a garden for creativity. The keystrokes were sounds of collective creation of a new future in concert.

The balance between this huge professional life and my family's life was like a high-wire act. Every decision was evaluated against the background of my beloved ones and their eyes. An investment of 1 lakh in our house wasn't a financial investment. It was a mooring and a guarantee of stability that I relied towards my entire family. It was a sign that, even as I reached toward the sky, my feet were grounded in the earth of our future together.

The freelance gig was my daily routine, a work but also a blessing. It allowed me to control my time in a world that offered nothing. But the guilt of a divided mind was always a shadow. The missed bedtime story to an appointment with a client, or the spreadsheet reviewed at the kitchen table, each seemed like a tiny crack within my soul. My role was mother, partner, daughter, and founder, and the symphony that accompanied these roles was usually an unsettling cacophony.

The trip was brutally sincere. A personal health issue added vulnerability to exhaustion. A financial snag could destroy our hard-earned stability, echoing past struggles in a brutal repeat of. There were moments when my entrepreneurial vision seemed like a gorgeous, massive burden that I could sink into.

However, in the connection between duty and ambition, I discovered my most profound truth. This wasn't just about survival, or even about the definition of success that society defines it. This was all about **growing.** It was about being able to prove that from the toughest ground, the most delicate and beautiful flowers could flourish. My professional growth and my family's warm embrace weren't opposing forces; they were twin suns that my life was now circling. Nurturing one is like taking care of the other, as they both grew up with the same passion: creating and providing significance.

As I end this chapter in my life, I think back on 2020, not as a time lost, but rather as an opportunity to find it. It was the year that the world fell apart, and in the cracks, I realized my own shining light. I discovered that resilience isn't an unfinished stone structure and an ever-bending willow tree through the storm, and yet never breaking, ever ready to grow to meet the rising sun. **Cominfo Source** stands today not as a tribute to my desires or to my will, but rather as a tribute to a love that dares to create a new future even in the autumn. It's my story that is not written in ink but through faith, A love story with potential that began when all was at a standstill, and my heart, despite all odds, chose to take off.

FINDING LIGHT IN THE STORM

I remember the silence most of all. It wasn't quiet, but a sigh of relief, an entire world trapped in a fragile glass of unknowing. Nashik - my hometown of ancient temples and vineyards was under a strange quiet, unspoken of. The bustling streets I had known as the tempo of my life had slowed to only a whisper. It was the year 2020, with humanity in the middle of a love-hate relationship with solitude. We were enamoured of the security of our homes, but we longed for the warmth of the world beyond. In this global moment, this collective breath and exhalation, I began the deepest love tale of my life. It was not with an individual, but with the prospect of. This is my story of the year, not written in ink but rather with electronic light and nerve endings, the story of a love story that is forged through determination and desperation.

The world I meticulously constructed disintegrated. As a young freelancer, the cafés, client conferences, and the like that made up my stage disappeared in a flash. The pandemic was a brutal editor, tearing out the physical pages of my professional experience. Panic Cold and slick was the first draft that I was unable to accept. I felt shackled, like a satellite without a connection to its orbit. In that space, I could hear an unsettling, new tune. It was the sound of a laptop or an online connection, and it was the sound from a distant future that was not closing, but changing.

I realised the truth that became my mantra an original quote born of necessity. I sang onto the four walls in my Nashik apartment: "The ground has not disappeared; it's just changed its shape. We now have to learn to dance on our feet in the air."

Freelancing evolved into an act of courtship between the invisible. Every video chat was an initial date; every email was a letter of love to a potential client. I was able to understand the language of bandwidth and pixels. My voice found warmth in frozen speakers. It wasn't a retreat; it was a revolt, an attempt to construct a fire in the middle of the storm. The problem was no longer concerned with finding work, but with the definition of what work should *be* like. It was a risk I had not anticipated in presenting my thoughts on a screen, and I hope it would resonate through the vastness.

When physical interactions became memories, the need for digital home stamps became imperative. It wasn't about a portfolio. It was about an actual *physical presence*. A persona. A lighthouse. The idea of constructing my own website as a refuge to house my marketing consulting began not as a business plan, but as an intense romantic desire. It was the desire to create something stunning and enduring from the void of worry that was circling me.

The process was incredibly imaginative; it was a courtship between my imagination and the empty screen. I would stay for a long time with the golden, soft glow of the evenings in Nashik spilling onto my desk, splattering the room with shades of resolute and amber. The tranquillity of the city and its vineyards, tucked away in the midst of fruits under the sun, was a part of my design. I wanted the place to evoke the feeling of a tranquil space in a dense, chaotic forest, a clear place. The choice of fonts and colours was an emotional process; every stroke of a letter or shade of blue represented who I was and what I hoped to become.

There were nights when the code was like a tangled skein of wool that I couldn't unwind. The technical glitches made me cry; editing the content felt like rewriting my own personal story. However, as each issue was being solved, I became more in love with the process. The work I created was a testimony to living well and clearly in the midst of whispers.

Within this digital world, an additional, more primitive tale unfolded: a search for an anchor. The pandemic had thrown the father of my son, Srinivas, and me into a turbulent sea of uncertainty about housing. The search for a place to live was a moving metaphor. Virtual tours were like ghost stories that haunted places empty of soul. Viewings from a distance were awkward ballets, our smiles concealed under masks and our gazes searching not only for rooms but for an experience of safety.

The weight was enormous. Each rejection, each inadequate space, was like a closing, not only on a home but on stability. In the quiet hours of exhaustion, my father, a man with few but powerful words, would just rest with me. His silence was not devoid of emotion, but a stronghold. Then, he would provide his wisdom, the solitary idea that was the foundation of my life: "Beta," he stated with a soft voice, a steady stream, "it is not the burden that makes you break. It's always how you decide to take it."

He showed me the beauty of power. Being able to carry a load with grace is the most potent creative practice. It's about putting the yoke into a pattern and transforming the burden into knowledge. Our search for a home was no longer frantic, but an intentional trip. We weren't looking just for refuge from the storm as much as a place in which we could gather and enjoy the rain without fear.

Then it was as if the universe was aligning its beats. Two revelations came at the same time.

Then came the day of launch. When I hit "Publish" on my website, my hands began shaking. It was like sending a love note to the unknown. It was a mix of terror and exciting optimism. It is **my digital consultancy, my ideas transformed into tangible objects, and my professional soul revealed.** It was more than a mere service; it was a declaration. In a world where companies were struggling, I created a tiny, steady fire. It represented a fierce, optimistic love of the near future and a belief that in the midst of chaos, we could find meaningfulness.

Then, the discovery. We entered Mantra Montana not with hope, however, but with a dull familiarity. However, when the light hit the floor of the living room, there was a shift. It was not an ordinary flat. The room seemed to be breathing with us. The view promised sunrises, not only walls. In the calm certainty of that place, the year's chaotic energy finally subsided. The decision was quick and emotional, a "yes" that came from an inner place beyond reason. The moment I made it official was a sign of faith, and a tangible counterpoint for my online leap. One was a house for my hopes as well as the home of my heart. They were both acts of affection.

2020 didn't provide me with any romantic partners according to the usual sense. It provided me with something much more fundamental: a deep love affair with my own ability to endure and be creative. I became enthralled by the adaptability and the graceful dancing of adapting. I was captivated by the gentle force of my father's strength and an ancestor's love story and grace honed over time. I became enthralled with the process of creating an online presence, a home, a brand-new version of me.

It was a concert of extreme, conflicting emotions of fear and confidence, as well as despair and hope, loneliness and deep connection all at once. I discovered that love isn't only a feeling that you feel for other people; it's the word we use to describe our lives. It's the way we **look after our dreams, care** for our hopes, **nurture** our ability to endure, **build** our refuges and **take on** your burdens in grace.

This is the story of the love that I have for you. It was written in the code that made my website, in the signature of the lease for our apartment, in the quiet power of the mantra my dad used to tell me, and in the steadfast heartbeat of Nashik, which stayed with me through. The pandemic was the furnace, but the fierce, inventive, and eternal passion for life was the alchemical process. This is a story that I have learned that will never stop.

"We are not the survivors from the tsunami. We are artists who learnt to paint using the rain and to build by the winds. Our refuge isn't in tranquillity; however, it is created from chaos."

DREAMS AND HEARTBREAK

The journey of parenthood, as I've discovered, isn't an objective, but rather an experience of the heart. It is a terrain shaped by hope, then eroded by despair, where the weather may change from a gentle spring of hope to the abrupt, brutal winter of grief in one breathless moment. It is our trek through that landscape, a story not of a single person but of a relationship that was tested and rebuilt through the fire of desire. It's the tale of Srinivas and me, of starlit choices and quiet tears, and of a minimal, fluttering existence that changed the landscape of our lives. The path we took wasn't the one we mapped, and it took us to a profound and well-worn fact: ***"Love is not just the basis on which you construct families; it's the compass you hold on to when the map is dissolved in your grasp."***

The decision to start was written in the peaceful language of our unity. It was born out of conversations that took place under the shade of stars from the past, and our voices weaving dreamlike tales into the darkness. It was born in the early morning hours, in the calming silence before the world began to wake, with shared smiles announcing a bright future and the thumping of tiny feet. Two souls joined by the years of love, and looking to weave an additional third of the threads of our love. It was an artist's desire to create something amazing and a testament to our union.

I can recall the night I spoke to the desire. Autumn's light was low in the blaze and set the world with crimson and gold. Looking towards Srinivas, I carry a vulnerable bird in my chest. I told him, "I think it's time we breathe new life into the globe." These words were hung between us, filled with excitement and anxiety. In his gaze, I saw my own dreams reflected in the magnificence of the unconditional love that was always our home. This dream was more than just a child; it offered healing, renewal and the enlargement of the world we created for two.

Then came the anticipation. A dark, cyclical expectation that increased with each passing month, only to be destroyed by the brutal, clinical negative of an unplastic stick. The joy of our first day gradually gave way to a quiet, anxious routine. Each failure was added to the grave we had erected, unnoticed by the outside world. The dreams of stars started to sound like echoes in an empty room.

In my desperate search, I was in desperate need of a modern talisman in the form of **The Inito fertility tracker**. The sleek device was more than a circuit and plastic. It was a beacon in our darkness, a symbol of our active pursuit within the slumber of waiting. It provided us with data charts, data, and a sense of control during a process that was profoundly mystical and inaccessible. For three months, it was the centre of our prayers and determination, a tiny altar of technology that we placed our trust in.

Then the month of November. A morning filled with pauses and incredulous eyes. The result was more than a line; it was dams breaking and releasing the joy of a flood so mighty it was dizzying. I wept and laughed, and, sighing, the burden of months of waiting slipped into the void in a split second. After meeting Srinivas, I was unable to speak. "We achieved this!" was the only expression I could come up with for our fight, and I sucked it out before falling into his arms. My arms were like the wall of a brand-new kingdom. We sat there, the rulers of a regal secret realm, convinced the most challenging part was in front of us.

Parenthood, we were reminded, is a tale of continuous change. Our story, so light-hearted, was shattered by a subtle, dark shadow. An ordinary blood test was the routine issue of a physician, and our world was swayed. High fasting sugar levels. Gestational diabetes. The words were cold and inaccessible, but the implications were clearly evident.

In the office of a doctor, the phrases "risk," "preeclampsia," "macrosomia," and "stillbirth" fell like hail and pockmarked the perfect scene of our happiness. It was a sensation to feel the blood drain out of my face, with a numb coldness settling in. Srinivas's hand was affixed to mine; his grip was tight and secure, the only solid object in the room, rapidly spinning. The dream that felt so real was now encased in the midst of medical hazard.

We rallied, as partners do. We became one group of management consultants, changing the kitchen area into a nutrition pharmacy and tracking our numbers with enthusiasm, replacing our prior charts. I was a frog of a stroll and greenery, my body became an edifice under careful, frightened remodelling. In my emotional state, it was like a pendulum moving from unwavering optimism to utter despair when I saw an irregular number on a glucose monitor. Through all of it, Srinivas was my steady ground. His affection was not only in the form of roses, but also in the careful way he prepared my lunch, the gentle reminders to check, and the silent, steady presence with me at each appointment.

However, medicine isn't the stuff of fairy tales. As the number of appointments increased and the news became grimmer. The dangers to the tiny existence within me, as well as to my own health, were growing beyond my ability to manage. We were offered a variety of alternatives, each covered in various shades of sadness. Then, the most unimaginable option was presented to us in the form of medical termination.

The following days were a blur of slumbering nights and tears-soaked silences. We sat in a circle and held on to hope as if we were standing on a cliff's edge, our fingers sliding. We were confronted by a complex decision-making process that was the overwhelming love for the child we'd already enumerated within our own hearts to be weighed against the horrifying chance of their suffering or being brutally cut short. Our dreams from laughter in hallways of our first days at school or of a portrait of the family were squiggled at the edges like burning paper.

The choice, at the time it was made, was not made out of surrender, but instead of the most devastating, protective love. It was the most agonising experience I've ever had and carved the deepest pit in my soul. In the midst of two years and 15 days of carrying the burden of life, it was decided to end it to prevent it from a future of suffering. It was a gesture of love that, at the moment, felt like destruction.

The process in Cloud Nine Hospital was a research study into sterile sorrow. It was an experience that felt physical, but a faint thing in comparison with the emotional cataclysm. While lying on that bed, I felt a portion of me disappearing slowly, forever. The world was quiet. Following the incident, the heavy, oppressive cloud fell over our house. Grief was our sole permanent guest around our kitchen table and lying on our sleeping.

We were ghosts in the places in which joy once lived. Conversations were dangerous, and silence was a suffocating cover. I sank into a pool of my own inadequacy and sadness, and Srinivas, in a beautiful but naive effort to be strong for me, fled into the safety of a quiet fortress of resilience. When his tears fell, he was in the darkness, alone. We were a small island in the same sea of loss, but we could not build bridges.

The bond that was our compass was now broken. In the evenings, we sat in separate chairs; the ticking of the clock was a mockery of our vision of the future. Misunderstandings bloomed like poisonous flowers. A comment on dinner could turn into a volcano of rage and fear. We were raw, and in our vulnerability, we harmed each other.

A fateful night, following an argument that was sparked by everything and nothing that was in the air and shook the room: separation. The once unfamiliar word was now in the middle of us, in a way that was ugly and utterly definitive. We looked at it, and then at one another as we surveyed the size of the chasm that had been opened. We had lost a child, and we were now in the midst of losing one another.

In the darkness that followed, my instinct came in. I couldn't be silent in our house in mourning. Therefore, I began walking. Every morning, as a dry winter morphed into an uncertain spring, I ventured into the park. I walked among the clump of leaves and skeletal trees, and their starkness reflected my heart. However, with every step, something changed. The tempo of the movement changed into an exercise in meditation. I observed the first flower bud, feisty, on a branch. I heard the bird's return song. The cycle continued at a beautiful, constant tempo, indifferent to my suffering.

The physical process of moving forward, step by step, became an image my soul understood. I wasn't moving ahead; I was moving *through*. In the quiet awe of nature's resiliency, I found an ounce of myself.

Slowly, slowly, I began reaching out to Srinivas's hands, but not in joyful sharing, but instead in shared devastation. We started to discuss, not about our future, but instead about the present pain. We renamed our sorrow in the name of our son, and spoke the name we imagined to each other with tears. We shared our fears, our fears of failure, and our fearful solitude *in* the relationship. We smashed down the fortresses, one brick at a time.

The way back to one of the other wasn't straight. It took a lot of patience. Needed to learn from scratch, as well as a vulnerability that was unsafe. We needed to rediscover the language we use to communicate, touching each other's shoulders, and a shared experience that was not connected to loss, a quiet tea that was made just as the other would like it.

For us, parenthood isn't a chapter that we've finished. It's a bond we cherish, one that took a form we never imagined, more painful. The child we imagined lives in the shadows of possibility, an unspoken, beloved part of the story of our relationship.

However, in the midst of that dark winter, another kind of family is emerging. It's a family of two that has been forever altered and scarred, but secured. We discovered that love isn't the absence of storms but rather the battered, strong vessel you create to navigate them. Our dream of sharing disappeared, but it changed. It lives on in the deepened compassion in Srinivas's eyes as I am held by him, in his fervent, hushed gratitude for a simple, healthy, happy day, in the promise to be grateful for the life we've created together, and for the elements we had in mind to add.

Our trip showed us that the most enlightening biographies aren't those that lack tragedy, but rather those in which love refuses to be its victim. The heart's terrain is more complex now, marked by an ebb and flow of loss, as well as the mighty, unshakeable mountains of a relationship that fought back. The future is still unpainted, but we have the brush in our hands today, with our hands held steady, with our colours blending not only with hope but also with the hard-earned gold of resiliency. The story of our family continues, evidence that sometimes your strongest family is the one that holds the light for one another long after the stars you had hoped for have disappeared.

THE BREAKING POINT

"Some love isn't meant to last forever; they are intended to be the crack that your own shining light finally, and painfully and achingly, comes out. The work we performed was an unfinished masterpiece and a symphony that had one missing movement, but beautiful, not for its resolution, but for the profound silence that accompanied the most profound note."

It is more than the story of loss. It's a story about a love I have for Srinivas and the child we had hoped to see, an affection that initially deepened, later testified, and then transformed by a loss that sat in silence and left a loud silence in its wake. This is not a way to blame anyone, as there are no villains in grief or shattered survivors. I write this to map the path of a heart that cried, broke and then learned to beat and beat again in a different way.

Our story began with the pigment of laughter shared and deep compassion. Srinivas was more than just my husband; he was my home away from home. The house we shared was a symphony of tapestries woven with a mix of inside jokes and planned futures, and the calming tranquillity of the synchronised silence. We created a universe within four walls that was impervious. When we heard of my pregnancy, it felt as if a fresh, vibrant colour had been added to our colour palette. We talked in quiet, striking hues of name, the first steps, of what the new person would be. It was no longer a vague notion; it was an actual, glowing promise tucked inside me. It was, in all ways, the architect of a collective dream.

Our loss of a child was like a seismic event that didn't produce any sound. In one moment, we were building castles in the air. But the next thing we knew, the ground under our collective life was gone. It was acute, single pain, but that was the psychological loss that created our new, oppressive environment. We were grieving the loss of a lifetime of events that were never to be, the first day of school with scraped knees and singing lullabies in the dark. The dreams were not gone, but they had been cut off and left phantom, raw arms of hope.

In the midst of the tragedy, our love, which had always sounded the same, began to split into dialects of sorrowful solitude. My grief was a stream that was seeking an outlet and needed to express itself in words, crying in urgent need to be felt and heard. I was compelled to speak our child's name aloud to make their short existence tangible in the world of memories.

But Srinivas? His sorrow was the size of a glacier. Huge, vast and reversing to the side. He was secluded in a fortress of quiet, a pragmatic body of working and fixing household objects and staring at the screens. While I saw his silence as a sign of abandonment, he probably considered my tears a deep well that he could never fill. The gap in our emotional lives was not just a blank space; it quickly filled with the heavy, cold water of miscommunication. I mistook his quiet for indifference. I think he mistook my desire to be a burden he could not endure.

Our house, once an oasis, was now an exhibition of our suffering. Ghosts haunted every room. The door to the nursery remained closed and silent, a testament to our lack of success. The kitchen table, at which we would once eat food and dreams, turned into the setting for standoffs that were silent, with the clinking of knives the only talk. The living room did not offer the comfort of the sofa, but rather a carefully planned distance from it.

Unspoken resentments started to form. We weren't Srinivas and I, a couple against each other. We were unwitting enemies, privately blaming each other, possibly even blaming each other. The grief altered our perceptions. When he returned home late from work, an attempt to soothe his grief in the solitude of his home, I felt in my raw heart as if he had abandoned me. He felt my suggestion to talk about our feelings like the need to heal an injury he was surgically seeking to recover.

The argument started and did not revolve around the massive, unknown, unimaginable problem, but rather around the dishes, the bills, or the tone of voice. They were proxy wars, the only weapons for our unspoken pain. The bitterness and love between us led to a tense battle for supremacy within our own walls. We were all drowning in the same sea; however, instead of keeping each other afloat, we mistook our floats for attacks.

The night I heard his conversation with his brother was when the trust glass was broken. The silence of the house amplified his exhausted, angry voice. "She does not understand," he said, and at that exact moment, I felt a loss that was so profound, it sucked away my breath. Our personal war was exported. My suffering, my struggle, was presented as an inability to understand *the man*. In the dark hallway, I felt a void that was more definite than anything I've ever felt. It was a realisation that the person I thought of as my home did not see me as a friend; instead, he saw me as an element of the encirclement.

If I had to confront him, I felt like an angry bird bouncing around my ribs. "I saw your voice," I said, the words hung in the air as if the verdict. I wasn't seeking a fight; I was looking for an open bridge, any indication that he could still see *us* under the rubble. His response, a slack, uninterested "What would you like me to tell you?" was colder than any anger. The sound was that of an emotional exile. The eyes of his were once warm pools, where I would love to swim, but had become shuttered, secluded windows. My beloved friend was so deep in his own demise that I was unable to reach him.

In the midst of our crisis, my parents appeared as a cavalry of concern. Their love was evident; however, their approach, rooted in the traditional endurance of marriage at all costs, became a new burden. Their rants about "harmony" or "working to sort things out" seemed like the script of a production that had already ended. As they expressed their fears, Srinivas's silence grew rigid, and my defences grew stronger. The external pressure didn't bring us together; it widened the distance between us, resulting in an open-air spectacle. In the midst of this well-meaning attack, I experienced an epiphany: healing was not governed through external pressures. My way forward was to be mine.

The decision to go wasn't a single moment; however, it was a gradual, painful dawn. This was the moment when we realised that by remaining, we were contributing to the slow, collective loss of the beautiful, loving people we once were. Love shouldn't be a war. We were two souls in mourning who were once a part of each other, but are now in a position not to be one another's source of salvation. We were pouring all of our strength into a vessel which was no longer able to hold it.

The process of packing my possessions was like an archaeology of an ancient civilisation. Every book he gave me, a picture of a vacation in the sun, and the blanket I'd hiddenly purchased for the baby were treasured relics. My hands were shaking as I rolled not just clothes, but entire chapters of my life.

The moment of saying goodbye was the most peaceful, the most deafening of all. He was standing by the door, a sculpted image of the person I loved. The air was filled with every spoken "I am in love with you," all "I'm sorry", and "what would happen." I didn't use them to express my feelings. I could see his eyes, at last, the reflection of my own deep sadness, not for the end of the world, but rather for the gorgeous, fragile, fragile thing that was damaged beyond our capacity to fix.

"Goodbye, Srinivas," I said. It wasn't an accusation. The release was to him and for me.

Moving away from the home was like walking off the edge of a cliff. The world outside was overwhelming, terrifying and bleak. However, as I drove away with tears obscuring the roads I once enjoyed so much, I noticed a solitary small sliver of light swing across the surface in my heart. It was the tiniest and terrifying light of possibility.

Our romance did not survive. However, a deeper, personal tale began to emerge from its detritus. I carried the bond of love that we shared, and the loss of our child, inside me, and not in the form of a wound but as a sacramental proof of my own ability to be a loving person. The silence that ruined us ultimately taught me to listen to my heart. The loneliness brought me back to my inner self.

Srinivas, I will always be grateful to the man you were when we first met. I'm sorry for the man you became after our break-up. We weren't sufficient to bear the grief of one another, which is perhaps the most humane of all. Our story shows that the final goodbyes can be the most powerful act of love. It was with a painful decision to end the bleeding, so that both souls could be given the chance to heal on their own and begin to love again in a new way in a better place under a brighter sky.

REBUILDING FROM RUINS

"Some affections aren't designed to last forever. They are, but they're necessary storms. They wash the dirt of your soul to ensure that you can experience new, more authentic things that can emerge."

The story of my heart is not a simple one. It is not a straight path through sun-dappled woods, but a journey that plunged, without warning, into a profound and terrifying cave, where the only light was that which I learned to carry within myself. To write it now is to trace my fingers over old scars and feel not just the remembered pain, but the astonishing resilience of the flesh that healed around it. This is the biography of a great love, and its greater undoing.

My journey with Srinivas began in the gentle, optimistic hues of a painting. Over the course of two years, we created an entire world. It was a place where mornings were shared, quiet conversations over hot cups of chai, hands entwined under restaurant tables, and the utter satisfaction of a familiar breath in the darkness. We created a language of glances, an era of jokes inside and a world that appeared to me to be secured and sacred. It was my belief in the structure of our union, its beams of trust and the wall of Respect for each other. I believed that it was a permanent home for my soul.

The incident wasn't shocking, and it wasn't an ominous confession or a found letter. Instead, it was an unassuming, simple statement spoken through the frozen phone, which is a modern-day dagger. "I have something that you must be aware of concerning Srinivas." His voice sounded quiet, but those eight words carried the power of an epoch that was about to end. In that instant, the ground that had been a part of my life was shattered. I was free-falling, holding the phone like it was the final rope that was fraying to my previous life.

The proof, when I looked it up, was a meticulous and brutal report. The dates on his calendar that were once harmless "work dinner", "client gathering" are now linked with alarming accuracy to his mysterious absences. Every detail was a slicing and a deliberate re-evaluation of my world. I would sit for hours with the glimmer of my smartphone reflecting the tears I was not feeling, dropping, trying to piece together the pieces of a different life that he was living. The man I left in the morning had become an unknown person by the time night fell. It was like I was reading a harrowing and erotic story about my husband. I'm playing the foolish, oblivious wife.

The psychological landscape within me transformed into a scene of unpredictable, violent weather. The initial shock, a cold, crippling numbness, was replaced by rising hot anxiety. The rage grew into an invisible tornado and swept away the shards of our wedding-day past, and when our son was born, we took a vacation in Goa, where he hugged me as we enjoyed the sunset. These very memories were soiled, their gold leaf peeling away to reveal the decaying wood underneath. What could the hands that were holding our son's newborn have been drawing the lines of a woman's face? This question was an enraged echo, a taunt to my head's cathedral.

It was like walking involuntarily into the midst of a fire. The distance between our living room, at first an inviting, familiar space, became a tense, terrifying gulf. The air got thicker and pressed against my lungs. My voice, as it came, was a foreign instrument that was shattered due to the pressures of a loss that was so profound that it was a volume of its own.

"Why?"

This one, simple, ancient query. It was a haze high in the sky, carrying numerous. What is the reason? What's the reason? Why would we want to destroy the foundations we've constructed? What made me choose to shatter my world? His eyes, those eyes I'd loved for the rest of my life, swung away, unable to take the ugliness of my sorrow. The answer he gave, as it finally came out in the simplest of all possible rebuttals: "It didn't mean anything."

The four words that followed were more tragic than the declarations of love. They implied that a great romantic love had not slain him. Instead, they had recklessly, unintentionally, thrown our precious history into the water to get something *that was of no value*. It was the most significant devaluation. He didn't trade our silver in exchange for gold. He had exchanged it for a cheap, shiny foil.

I presented my evidence, not in anger but with deep, calm sorrow. Each day, each moment that I presented was a solitary point in our relationship's coffin. I watched him sag his excuses, anxiety and loneliness, a flash of rage that sounded like a hollow gourd. This was not a battle about finding facts. The facts were already out there, solid and cold. It was about something completely different: the ritual of removing knots from our souls. The idea was standing among the ruins and declaring that with every trembling ounce of my body, "I am here. I can see this. It is not my intention to let this abomination have a home."

In the days that followed, a bizarre duality took over. By day, I was a solitary ghost who managed households and joked with children, and inside, a mute scream echoed endlessly. In the evening, in the quiet, the clarity of a new day emerged out of the chaos. It was a numb surgical clarity. I realised that the affection I was holding onto was not a present-tense reality, but rather a haunting, beautiful memory. The man I adored was gone, replaced by this savvy con artist.

The divorce decision did not come in one flash of thunder; it came as a dawning, like the gradual, unavoidable dawn after an extraordinarily long and tiring night. A sleepless night, as I was watching the moon's way across our bedroom floor, I was struck by the gleam of lightning: ***To remain is to teach my kids that love is the place of compromise, Respect isn't a prerequisite and that self-betrayal is the price to pay for tranquillity***. This realisation was my lighthouse. It wasn't just about my heart breaking, but about the blueprint for love I was leaving as a legacy.

It was like a dry bureaucratic response to the emotional calamity. It was about custody and assets, whereas my heart was filled with broken hopes and snatched futures. The society, with its snarling judgments and demeaning eyes, has often attempted to portray divorce as an unsatisfactory experience. But when I completed the divorce papers, holding my hand steady at the beginning of many months, I did not feel like a failure, but rather a powerful, frightening act of reconstruction. I wasn't destroying an entire family, but saving its remaining members from the wreckage of a ship.

Through it all, my family was my primary source of support. My father, who was a man with few words, discovered the right ones: "You are stronger than you think, Beta. Certain earthquakes aren't meant to drown us, but to show the rock below." They created my tears without letting me drown them. It was a reminder that the ending of a story is also a blank page to begin the next chapter.

The trip between "we" and back "I" is the most romantic journey of my life, not romantic by the definition of flowers and sonnets, but in the discovery of my personal soul. I've learned to befriend myself, to hear my own voice, to feel a sense of companionship within my own strength. The love story of my life did not end with Srinivas and his family; it just changed the protagonists. I'm now the lover and the loved and am learning the delicate, brutal art of self-devotion.

Srinivas and I wrote an incredibly heartfelt, beautiful poem at one time. However, a poem, no matter how beloved it is, should not be repeated forever when its meaning has diminished. Our vows have broken down, and they are now my own. I've made a new silent promise to myself never to forget to confuse love for comfort and history for destiny or the fear of loyalty.

The human heart functions as a marvellous organ. It doesn't just break. It *alters*. It gets used to an entirely new way, one that evokes the strength of survival and ultimately, a cautious, joyful, hopeful type of joy. The hurt of his infidelity is the flame that stoked my old independent self. In the ashes of that, I'm rising, not as an angry woman whose identity is defined by the loss of a loved one, but rather as an eagle made by me. My wings are embroidered with the threads of my grief as well as wisdom and an unshakeable, hard-earned peace. My story is no longer the story about "us." It's the real, unfolding tale about "me," and for the first time in a long, long time, I am reading a book I'm looking forward to reading.

From Darkness to Starlight

The day I signed my divorce papers, the ink didn't dry on legal parchment; it was absorbed into the paper of my soul, creating a permanent, trembling end to a chapter I had previously believed was the entire book. It was less the end of a story, more a brutal need to turn a page, the roughness of the paper rubbing my heart, the sound echoing through the ribs' hollow. I recall walking unintentionally until I reached an undiscovered park. As I sat on a bench in the sun, I listened to the squeals of children echo through the oak trees, a sound so pure it felt like a key. It opened a floodgate. Memories that were not about him, however, memories of the woman I was before becoming a wife, were neatly tucked away in my attic. She awoke, dusty with visions, eyes shining with the hope I'd since left. In the instant, I wasn't ending a relationship; I was forced to face the love affair that I had ignored for so long, and that was the one I had with myself.

"I discovered that love isn't always a symphony that can be played by two. Sometimes, the most powerful love story begins with a simple whisper in the darkness or a promise that you whisper to your eager hearts."

Society, the famous, silent writer, has written my character's narrative for me. The divorced woman was a paragraph that was unfinished or a sentence that faded into a stifling, pathetic silence. I felt it in receding invitations, and my presence was an awkward, single chair in a sea of mixed happiness. I felt it in the mute question that floated over the room, denser than the scent of perfume. *Was there something off?* The assumption is that something *was* wrong with me. In gatherings, I walked through an enigma of well-meaning words that were as sharp as glass. "You're amazing," they'd say, their eyes pleading for a donation that crushed my spirit. I wasn't brave, I was bleeding, and their eyes were like salt on the wound.

I went back to my childhood room at my parents ' house, which was a time capsule filled with lost dreams. My youth was a constant, aching presence. In the stillness of the night, when I drew in the patterns that I was familiar with on the ceiling at night, my mother's old words came back to me not as a warning, but rather as a saviour: "A tree does not mourn the fallen leaves shed, but it builds energy for the new growth." It was not too late. The soul's soil, even though it was bare, was not dead. With a determination rooted in pure desperation, I began the arduous, painful task of piecing together the person I intended to be. I began writing. It was, at first, an unspoken scream onto the paper, and a smattering of confusion and grief. The screams were transformed into words, the words into sentences, and the sentences began to weave my broken universe back together. Writing became my private rendezvous, my shady love letter to myself and my possibilities.

The catalyst was real during a day of rain, and the sky was the shade of old incense. Cleansing out my old laptop, an heirloom from times, I came upon a lost file and a half-written story from a decade ago. When I began to read my youthful prose, a light that had been dormant for a long time, flickered. It was a random thought driven by an impulse I could not comprehend. I responded to an informal request to submit articles to a tiny online journal. When I clicked the "send button, it was as loud as an emitted heartbeat. The simple email was a message inside a bottle being tossed into the digital sea. When I received a response, with an acknowledgement, that was much more than just an opportunity. It was a confirmation of my words, or my story was still important. It brought back a creative energy I had thought was dead.

Since then, writing stopped being an idle pastime. It was a form of revitalization. I began to entertain my own thoughts and to retell my personal memories. I wrote about the silence that remained after the door shut, about the weight of a wedding ring no longer on my finger, and about the frightful and exhilarating sensation of being alone. Through each essay, each vulnerable admission, I was regaining not only a skill but also a soul. I was adrift as I learned my own rhythms and my own depths, and eventually fell in love with the woman I met there.

Financial independence, once a common goal, became an intimate love song for survival. One of the first budgets I created on my own was a terrifying number sonnet, which was a scathing poem of need. But, in the confines of it, I discovered a surprising liberty. Every bill that I paid using my own money was a sign of empowerment. I learned to prioritize more than only utilities, but also joy in writing workshops here, and an uplifting book there. These were not frivolous; they were notes of love for my life to come.

My website, **"Every Life Matters,"** began as an unnamed, faceless place. However, as I put my heart into the pages of my blog, it happened remarkably, and it returned. Women across the world echoed, "Me too." They shared their stories interspersed with mine, creating a tapestry of shared strength. The therapy that began was transformed into an unanticipated source of income that was modest, however, mine. Through adverts and freelance gigs, my words started to nourish me, an incredible alchemy that transformed my emotions into strength.

The journey of self-romance was not one I walked alone. My family, following the initial shock, became my constant refuge. The place they called home served as my anchor, and they believed that what I could have was the wind that blew my sails. There were the unintentional suitors of the spirit friends, familiar and brand new. They walked in, not out of sympathy or pity, but in friendship. A former coworker who linked me to work as well as a reader who was a pen-pal, and someone who was a stranger at a coffee house, who was awed by my book that I had been writing about. These were my cupids in my return, launching connections that healed, not wounded.

Re-entering the world of work was a frightening courtship ceremony. I felt old, and my confidence was shaky. The rejections were like romantic rejections; each was a blow to my newly found confidence. But I persevered. I worked in the non-profit sector, an area where my passion could take me. While working on projects that helped children and women, I heard stories of strength that mirrored my own. As I helped single mothers get back on their feet and reaffirmed my personal. This was a passion with a purpose, a constant reminder that my suffering created a love that could inspire others.

In the quiet moments, I discovered the most intimate romantic love that I have ever experienced: the love for solitude. I'd lie awake, my doubts as cold as sheets. However, I was able to soothe them by taking my breath. I'd light a candle and make tea, and then sit in silence with my thoughts. In the silence, I began to pay attention to the gentle, authentic voice that was lost for a long time. I developed gratitude, not as a pious statement, but as a routine of looking at the sun's rays in the pages, the smell of rain, and the comfort of my own resiliency. I discovered that happiness isn't an endpoint to be achieved by another person, but rather the landscape that needs to be nurtured within.

As I write this love story of my life, I am feeling an overwhelming sense of returning home. The person who was in the park, shattered by loss, wouldn't be able to recognize me as the person that I am today. I am filled with a solitary, indefinable enthusiasm. My story isn't about what happened and the life I've tenderly and hard-fought to build on top of it.

The story of my life is made up of threads of gold and grief, reflecting loneliness and connections. The backdrop is the monsoons that engulf Pune and the eternal memories of Bhubaneswar, seasoned with memories of my mother's cooking, a love language that doesn't require translation. I've learned that the longest-lasting love stories do not always start with a romantic encounter. It could begin in a tranquil park during a rainy afternoon, under the gentle light of a laptop's screen after one brave choice to close the book and begin over.

"They said I was not complete. This led me to my own universe, spinning in dreams, enlightened by self-discovery and then gravitating toward my own radiant centre."

This is my story of love. It's messy, it's never-ending, and it's the most honest thing I've ever encountered. To anyone reading this and grieving endings, I tell you this: *your love story isn't over. It's just ready for you to grab the pen. Begin. Create a new chapter in your life. The most memorable chapter is the one that you dare to write next.*

About The Author

Sweta Leena Panda, an alumna of IIIT Bhubaneswar, is a multifaceted writer and professional, excelling in product marketing and project management. Since beginning her writing journey in 2012, she has crafted over 250 poems and numerous blogs, exploring themes of love, resilience, and the human spirit. A passionate traveller and social worker, Sweta's experiences shape her storytelling. Her upcoming novels, *Infidelity or Reality*, *The Underdog's Ascent*, and *Life Demands From My Older Self*, set to release in 2025, showcase her creative versatility.